Total Eclipse

by

CHRISTOPHER HAMPTON

FABER AND FABER
24 Russell Square
London

First published in 1969
by Faber and Faber Limited
24 Russell Square London WC1
Printed in Great Britain by
Latimer Trend & Co Ltd Plymouth
All rights reserved

SBN 571 08918 6 (*Cloth*)
SBN 571 09031 1 (*Paper Cover*)

822

ḤAM

TOTAL ECLIPSE

The first performance of *Total Eclipse* was given at the **Royal** Court Theatre on 11th September 1968. The cast was as follows:

MME MAUTÉ DE FLEURVILLE, Verlaine's mother-in-law	Kathleen Byron
MATHILDE VERLAINE, Verlaine's wife	Michele Dotrice
ARTHUR RIMBAUD	Victor Henry
PAUL VERLAINE	John Grillo
CHARLES CROS	Malcolm Ingram
M. MAUTÉ DE FLEURVILLE	Nigel Hawthorne
ÉTIENNE CARJAT	Nigel Hawthorne
ERNEST CABANER	William Hayland
JEAN AICARD	Stanley Lebor
CLERK	Stanley Lebor
JUDGE THÉODORE T'SERSTEVENS	Nigel Hawthorne
EUGÉNIE KRANTZ	Ursula Smith
ISABELLE RIMBAUD, Rimbaud's sister	Gillian Martell
A BARMAN	William Hoyland
MAID	Judy Liebert

Artists, customers in cafés etc.

Directed by Robert Kidd
Designed by Patrick Procktor

ACT 1

5

INTERVAL

ACT 2

FOR HARRY AND LYNN

'Die blaue Blume richtet sich nach den Jahreszeiten. Heinrich vernichtet diesen Zauber—zerstört das Sonnenreich.'

NOVALIS: Paralipomena to *Heinrich von Ofterdingen*

ACT ONE

Scene 1

The Paris home of M. Mauté de Fleurville; 10th September, 1871. The drawing-room of a wealthy bourgeois household. It is furnished in a vaguely Louis XV style, not particularly tasteful, a certain amount of red and yellow velvet. There are two doors. In one corner of the room a multitude of bell-pulls of various lengths and styles in gaudy colours. There are family portraits and mirrors on the walls, and various porcelain ornaments, crucifixes and other objects scattered about the room. There is also a grand piano.

At this, MME MAUTÉ DE FLEURVILLE *is sitting, when the curtain rises. She is playing the closing bars of a piano transcription of the Prelude to 'Lohengrin'. She is a middle-aged woman, quite elegantly dressed.* MATHILDE VERLAINE *enters, carrying a bunch of flowers which she begins arranging in a vase. She is an attractive girl of 18, now 8 months pregnant.*

As MME M. DE F. *is coming to the end of the piece, a strange and incongruous figure enters the room, and stands for a moment, waiting in the shadows, so that neither of the women notice him. It is* ARTHUR RIMBAUD. *His appearance is striking. He is not quite 17, and looks his age. His hands are large and dirty. His tie looks like a piece of old string and hangs loose around his neck, the collar-button open. Despite all this he is extremely good-looking in a cruel sort of way; thin lips, cold, grey eyes. When he speaks it is with a light and indefinable provincial accent.* MME M. DE F. *finishes playing.*

RIMBAUD : Evening.

The women both jump. MATHILDE *all but knocks over the vase.*)
I'm looking for M. Paul Verlaine.
(*Silence.*)

MME M. DE F. (*as if she didn't believe it*) : Are you . . . M. Rimbaud?

9

RIMBAUD: Yes.

MME M. DE F.: Er, M. Rimbaud, I am Mme Mauté de Fleurville, M. Verlaine's mother-in-law. And this is Mme Verlaine, my daughter.

(RIMBAUD *smiles frostily and nods to the two women.*)

You're not with M. Verlaine?

RIMBAUD: No.

MME M. DE F.: Only . . . he went to the station to meet you. I suppose, er, he must have missed you.

RIMBAUD: Yes. Well, he doesn't know what I look like, does he?

MME M. DE F.: We're expecting him any minute.

(*Silence.*)

Er, how did you get here?

RIMBAUD: Walked.

MME M. DE F.: Oh, it's quite a long way.

RIMBAUD: Not really.

(*Silence.*)

MME M. DE F.: Perhaps you'd like a wash after your long journey.

RIMBAUD (*considers this a moment*): No thanks.

MME M. DE F.: Well, did you give your luggage to one of the servants?

RIMBAUD: I didn't meet any servants.

MME M. DE F.: Did you leave it in the hall then?

RIMBAUD: What?

MME M. DE F.: Your luggage.

RIMBAUD: I haven't got any luggage.

MME M. DE F.: No . . . luggage?

RIMBAUD: No.

MME M. DE F.: Oh.

(*Silence.*)

MATHILDE: Won't you sit down, M. Rimbaud?

(RIMBAUD *sits down, and the women follow suit. By now the atmosphere is extremely sticky.*)

MME M. DE F.: I don't suppose M. Verlaine will be long.

(RIMBAUD *produces a repulsive old clay pipe from an inside pocket and lights it.*)

RIMBAUD: Mind if I smoke?

MME M. DE F. (*with obvious distaste*): Er, no, not at all.

(*Silence.*)

M. Verlaine and I were very impressed by your poetry.

RIMBAUD: Did you read it, too?

MME M. DE F.: Oh, yes. I'm a fervent admirer of the Muse. Of course, my talents are principally musical (*she giggles*), but I've always had a soft spot for poetry. We're great friends with M. Victor Hugo, you know. He's an utterly charming gentleman.

RIMBAUD: He's getting a bit senile.

MME M. DE F.: I don't think so. He still has perfect command of his faculties.

(RIMBAUD *smiles.*)

Naturally to the young he seems a little . . . elderly. But then the young must always be revolutionary. That's why M. Verlaine and I were so impressed with your talent. It must be wonderful to be such a talented young man.

MATHILDE: You're even younger than we thought you were.

MME M. DE F.: All the more impressive.

MATHILDE: How old are you?

MME M. DE F.: Darling, it's not very polite to ask people their ages.

MATHILDE: I'm sorry. I was just . . . so interested.

(*She looks inquiringly at* RIMBAUD, *but he chooses to ignore her question and gets up, moving over to look out of the window.*)

RIMBAUD: Pleasant view.

MME M. DE F.: Yes, charming, isn't it?

RIMBAUD: Pleasant.

(RIMBAUD *picks up a china animal and considers it with distaste. He moves over into a corner, looking for somewhere to knock out his pipe. With a deft movement he flicks the ash out into a bowl which, as we can tell from Mme M. de F.'s agitated reaction, is obviously not intended for such a use. At this moment* PAUL VERLAINE *enters. He is an exceptionally ugly man with a face like a fat skull. He is 27, bearded, but already almost bald. He is well-dressed and looks like a minor civil servant with private means—which is what he is. He doesn't notice* RIMBAUD, *who is standing looking out of the window.*)

11

VERLAINE: No sign of him. Cros and I combed the station, but in vain. Still, no doubt he'll get here in the end.

RIMBAUD (*without turning round*): He's here.

VERLAINE (*spinning round*): M. Rimbaud?

(*He advances to shake hands with* RIMBAUD, *than as* RIMBAUD *turns towards him, he pauses for a moment, apparently surprised by* RIMBAUD'*s appearance.*)

RIMBAUD: M. Verlaine.

VERLAINE: You found your own way here. What initiative.

MME M. DE F.: Where's Cros?

VERLAINE: Oh, he's pottering around downstairs somewhere. He'll be up soon.

MME M. DE F.: Good, well, if we're all here I must see about organizing some dinner. I expect M. Rimbaud must be hungry.

RIMBAUD: Starving.

MME M. DE F.: Yes . . . well, I'll see what we can arrange. (*To* MATHILDE.) Come along, dear. You can give me a hand and the men can have a little chat.

(*Exit* MME M. DE F. *and* MATHILDE.)

VERLAINE: Well, it's really very nice to meet you.

(RIMBAUD *nods. He is clearly relieved by the departure of the women.*)

VERLAINE: How old are you, if you don't mind my asking?

RIMBAUD: I do.

VERLAINE: Oh, sorry.

RIMBAUD: Sixteen.

VERLAINE: Sixteen? Are you sure?

RIMBAUD: Of course I'm sure.

VERLAINE: It's just that you said in your letter that you were twenty-one.

RIMBAUD: You never want to believe what I say in my letters.

VERLAINE: I'm amazed. I thought those poems you sent me were remarkable for someone of twenty-one: for someone of sixteen, they're incredible.

RIMBAUD: That's why I told you I was twenty-one. I didn't want you to feel condescending before you'd read them.

VERLAINE: Of course, it all becomes clearer now. The fact that

12

your mother kept you at home with no money. If you're
sixteen. You've left school, have you?

RIMBAUD: Yes.

VERLAINE: I suppose your mother must be very angry with me.

RIMBAUD: No, once she found out you'd sent me my train fare
she seemed quite happy.

VERLAINE: Don't you get on with her?

RIMBAUD: I wouldn't mind if she was just stupid. All the rest of
my family are stupid, and they're perfectly acceptable. But
she's religious as well. Bigoted.
(*Silence.*)

VERLAINE: Do you like it here?

RIMBAUD: It's not quite . . . what I'd expected.

VERLAINE: How do you mean? (*Pause.*) Oh, I see. Well, I'm not
really the garret type. My wife and I did have a flat on the
Quai de la Tournelle when I was working. But what with one
political upheaval and another, I decided I was too sensitive
for the Civil Service. So I couldn't afford to keep on the flat.
Then Mathilde's father, rot his guts, very generously
offered to let us have a floor of this house. I thought it
would be quite a good idea, Mathilde being pregnant and
everything.

RIMBAUD: And wasn't it?

VERLAINE: Yes, yes, except for my loathsome father-in-law.
Fortunately for you, he's away at the moment. On a
shooting party. Where I sincerely hope he will meet with a
fatal accident. My daily devotions are entirely directed to
that end.

RIMBAUD: What does he do?

VERLAINE: Nothing. He's a gentleman of leisure. And he does
absolutely nothing. He's the most pointless person I know.
His sole purpose in life is to die and leave me all his money.
What do you think of my wife?

RIMBAUD: Your wife?

VERLAINE: Yes.

RIMBAUD: Well, I haven't had much time to judge, have I?

VERLAINE: I suffered for that girl, you know. I had to wait over
a year before I could marry her. The fates were against the

13

marriage. It was delayed so many times. By pestilence and war. Literally. She caught smallpox at the last minute, I thought Mary mother have I waited all this time to get married to a flayed hedgehog? Fortunately she was quite unmarked. Then two days before the wedding, one of my best friends committed suicide which I felt betrayed a certain lack of tact. The next day, the final indignity, I got called up. But I was immune to all the portents, I even squirmed out of that—and I married her. Alas, I heeded not the warnings of the Gods.

I'm very fond of her really. It's just that living with her parents has a bad effect on her. And being pregnant. She's only a child.

RIMBAUD: So am I.

(*Enter* CHARLES CROS, *29, a languid dandy, with frizzy hair and a lugubrious moustache.*)

CROS: Ah, you must be Rimbaud. Nice to meet you.

VERLAINE: Rimbaud, this is Charles Cros, inventor.

CROS: And poet.

VERLAINE: And poet.

CROS: I'm glad you managed to find your way here. No thanks to this drunken oaf. I couldn't understand why he was so keen to come and meet you until we got outside the door. Any excuse to get out for a few drinks. You see what a terrible thing it is to be married.

VERLAINE: It's all lies.

CROS: The thing was, your train arrived at the emerald hour. The hour of absinthe.

I liked your poems.

RIMBAUD (*to* VERLAINE): Have you shown them to everyone?

VERLAINE: No, why?

RIMBAUD: Your mother-in-law just complimented me on them.

VERLAINE: Really? Deceitful old hag. I only showed her one.

RIMBAUD: Which one?

VERLAINE: The clean one.

RIMBAUD: Ah.

CROS: I loved that one about the girl spending the night before her first communion in the lavatory with a candle. My

14

word. Magnificent stuff.

RIMBAUD (*coldly*): What do you invent?

CROS: Well, if you mean what am I inventing at the moment, I can't really tell you, because it hasn't been invented.

RIMBAUD: What have you invented?

CROS: Nothing really, I always seem to lose interest. Or run out of money.

VERLAINE: Ah, but this time he's on to something really good.

RIMBAUD: What?

VERLAINE: Photographs with colour. You explain.

(*Enter* MME M. DE F. *and* MATHILDE. RIMBAUD *fills and relights his pipe.*)

CROS: Are you interested in photography?

RIMBAUD: No.

MATHILDE: You're not talking about that again, are you Cros?

CROS: It wasn't I who brought the subject up, Madame.

MATHILDE: I don't know why you didn't stick to jewellery.

VERLAINE (*to* RIMBAUD): Cros created a perfect ruby. Absolutely indistinguishable from a genuine ruby.

RIMBAUD: That should make you some money.

CROS: Unfortunately not. My ruby cost considerably more to make than a mere genuine ruby.

MME M. DE F.: We should be able to have dinner soon.

RIMBAUD: Good. I'm famished.

(*Silence.*)

MME M. DE F.: You come from the Ardennes, don't you, M. Rimbaud? Charleville?

RIMBAUD: Yes.

CROS: Pleasant town, Charleville, isn't it?

RIMBAUD: The last place on God's earth.

CROS: Oh.

MATHILDE: And what does your father do?

RIMBAUD: I believe he confines himself principally to drinking. I can't say with any certainty though, because he was wise enough to leave my mother some ten years ago, and we haven't seen him since.

MATHILDE: Oh . . . I'm sorry.

RIMBAUD: No need to be. He's very well out of it.

15

(*Silence.*)

MME M. DE F. (*coming to the rescue again*): I have an idea. Wouldn't it be nice to have a little poetry before dinner? I must confess, M. Rimbaud, that I misled you somewhat: M. Verlaine didn't let me see all your poems. Won't you read the others to us now?

MATHILDE: Oh, yes, that would be lovely.

MME M. DE F.: Can you fetch them for M. Rimbaud, Paul?

VERLAINE (*hesitating*): Er. . . .

RIMBAUD: No.

MATHILDE: Oh, why not?

RIMBAUD: I don't want to.

MME M. DE F.: M. Rimbaud is probably tired after his journey, dear. Perhaps some other time. . . .

RIMBAUD: No. I never read out my poetry.

CROS: Why not? I mean, if you've taken the trouble to write it, it seems strange to want to keep it to yourself.

MATHILDE: All the other poets do it. We have soirées and everybody reads.

RIMBAUD: I'm not interested in what all the other poets do.

CROS: I think you'd find it very instructive and useful. Don't you think poets can learn from one another?

RIMBAUD: Only if they are bad poets.

CROS: I see.

MATHILDE: I'm sure you'd enjoy our soirées. We had a lovely one last week. Poetry and music. Musset and Chopin.

RIMBAUD: Musset?

MATHILDE: Yes. My favourite poet. Except for Paul, of course. Don't you like Musset?

RIMBAUD: Slovenly facile rubbish. The most objectionable and least talented of all the miserable buffoons of this dreary century. A poet for women and schoolboys.

CROS: Ah, but what about his plays?

RIMBAUD: The theatre is beneath contempt.

CROS: Your opinions are firm.

RIMBAUD: Shouldn't they be?

(*A* MAID *enters.*)

MAID: Dinner is served, Madame.

16

MME M. DE F.: Ah, good. Shall we go in?

RIMBAUD (*to* VERLAINE): Look, I must have a piss before supper. Can you tell me where to find it?

(*The others exchange glances as* VERLAINE *murmurs directions. Exit* RIMBAUD.)

MME M. DE F.: Well.

CROSS: Extraordinary man.

MATHILDE: He's not how I imagined him.

VERLAINE: He's all right.

CURTAIN

Scene 2

The same; 25th September, 1871.

When the curtain rises, the stage is empty. Enter RIMBAUD *smoking his pipe. He pauses and looks around the room, then, after a moment's consideration, goes over and picks up the china animal which we have already seen him handle in Scene 1. He contemplates it briefly, then deliberately drops it on the floor and smashes it.*

Voices offstage. RIMBAUD *moves swiftly over to one of the doors and pauses there, waiting in the shadows. Enter* M. MAUTÉ DE FLEURVILLE *at the other door. He is an imposing man of 64, with a white beard. He is followed by the* MAID, *who carries his overcoat over her arm. Neither of them see* RIMBAUD.

MAID: We weren't expecting you back today, monsieur.

M. DE F.: Where is everyone? Where's my wife?

MAID: I think she's in the garden, monsieur. With Mme Mathilde.

M. DE F.: Would you go and tell them I'm back?

MAID: Yes, monsieur.

(M. DE F. *notices the broken china animal.*)

M. DE F.: What's this mess on the floor?

MAID: Oh, it's broken. (*She kneels down to gather up the pieces.*) I'm sorry, monsieur, I don't know what happened, it wasn't here when I came round.

M. DE F.: Hm. Bring me some coffee, will you?

MAID: Yes, monsieur.

(*She exits.* M. DE F. *sinks down on to the sofa, grunts. Silence.* RIMBAUD *reaches over to the door, opens it and closes it again.*)

RIMBAUD: Morning.

(M. DE F. *starts and turns round.*)

(*Hospitably.*) Everyone's out. They should be back soon.

Unless you've come to see the old boy.

M. DE F.: The old boy?

RIMBAUD: M. Mauté. De Fleurville. You're not a friend of his, are you?

M. DE F.: Er . . . no.

RIMBAUD: No, I didn't think you were. As far as I can gather he doesn't have any friends.

M. DE F. (*faintly*): Oh . . . really.

RIMBAUD: Yes. Apparently he defeats all comers with an impregnable combination of tediousness and avarice. It is darkly rumoured that he cannot resist rifling the pockets of those who fall stunned by the monotony of his anecdotes.

(M. DE F. *is beginning to show signs of impending fury. He utters one or two indeterminate sounds, but* RIMBAUD *interrupts him, suavely changing tack.*)

You wouldn't like to buy a crucifix, by any chance, would you? (*He produces one from an inside pocket.*) Because I happen to have one with me which I can let you have on extremely reasonable terms. It's ivory, I think.

(M. DE F. *stares at the crucifix, which he recognizes as his own, with rage and incomprehension.*)

Tempted?

(M. DE F. *rises to his feet.*)

M. DE F.: Who the hell are you?

RIMBAUD: I might ask you the same question. Except I'd be more polite.

M. DE F. I am Mauté de Fleurville.

RIMBAUD: Morning.

(*He exits smartly.* M. DE F. *gapes after him. He strides over*

18

to the other door, which opens before he reaches it. Enter
MME M. DE F. *and* MATHILDE.)

MME M. DE F.: Hello, dear!

M. DE F.: What's going on in this house?

MME M. DE F.: What do you mean?

M. DE F.: I've just been insulted by some scruffy fellow trying to sell me one of my own crucifixes.

MME M. DE F.: What?

M. DE F.: Some youth. . . .

MATHILDE: Rimbaud.

MME M. DE F.: He's a friend of Paul's. A poet. Paul invited him to come and stay for a bit.

M. DE F.: A poet?

MME M. DE F.: Yes. He sent Paul some poems, and said he wanted to come to Paris, but had nowhere to stay. So Paul offered to put him up here.

M. DE F.: Since when has Verlaine had the right to invite his wretched friends to stay in my house. Without my permission.

MME M. DE F.: Paul said he was a genius.

M. DE F.: I don't care if he is a genius. Doesn't give him the right to insult his betters.

MATHILDE: Get rid of him, Daddy.

M. DE F.: I have every intention of doing so.

MATHILDE: I don't like him. He's nasty and malicious.

MME M. D. F.: He's had a quite disastrous effect on Paul.

M. DE F.: What do you mean?

MATHILDE: He's changed completely since Rimbaud came.

MME M. DE F.: I'm sure he hasn't done a stroke of work for weeks. He's given up bothering about his clothes as well. And I think . . . he's probably been drinking more than is good for him.

M. DE F.: Oh, has he?

MATHILDE: It's all Rimbaud's fault.

M. DE F.: Nonsense. You know very well that Verlaine gives up working at the slightest excuse. Nevertheless, I shall send this person packing at once. For one thing, I'm not having anyone wandering round the house dressed like that. Makes

19

the place look like a workhouse.

MATHILDE: That's nothing.

MME M. DE F.: Yes, he's already scandalized the neighbours by sunbathing in the front garden.

M. DE F.: By doing what?

MME M. DE F.: Sunbathing in the front garden.

MATHILDE: With his shirt off.

M. DE F.: Why didn't you stop him?

MME M. DE F.: I tried to. I went out and told him that it wasn't really done in this area to sunbathe in the garden and he said, what a coincidence, it wasn't really done in Charleville either.

M. DE F.: Insolence.

MME M. DE F.: And then he said . . . do not disturb me, I am about my father's business. Pointing at the sun.

M. DE F.: Blasphemy.

MME M. DE F.: I think he was drunk.

MATHILDE: He's always drunk.

(*Enter* VERLAINE. *He has been drinking. He is a little taken a-back at the sight of* M. DE F. *His clothes, old, scruffy and baggy, contrast sharply with what he was wearing in the previous scene. He wears a battered felt hat.*)

VERLAINE: Ah.

(*He shakes hands warily with* M. DE F., *then turns away.*)

(*Muttering.*) Not even a flesh wound.

M. DE F.: Pardon.

VERLAINE: Nothing, nothing.

(*Silence.*)

M. DE F.: I have a bone to pick with you.

VERLAINE: Pick away.

M. DE F.: Since when have you had the right to invite people to stay here without my permission?

VERLAINE: Since you had the kindness to offer the second floor of your house to Mathilde and me, I've treated it as our home.

M. DE F.: So it is. Your home, not a guest house.

VERLAINE: If I can't put up one guest in my home when I feel like it, I might as well live somewhere else.

20

M. DE F.: If you weren't so idle, you might be able to afford to.

VERLAINE: Now listen, you know very well that after the Commune, it would be dangerous, if not impossible, for me to work at the office.

M. DE F. (*to the others*): Any excuse.

VERLAINE: I don't notice you working your fingers to the bone.

M. DE F.: How dare you?

MATHILDE: Don't talk to Daddy like that.

M. DE F.: Now, look here, Verlaine, I warn you. . . .

(*He breaks off abruptly as the* MAID *enters with a coffee tray.*)

MAID: Your coffee, monsieur.

M. DE F.: What?

MAID: Coffee. You asked me to bring it.

M. DE F.: Take it away, I don't want it.

VERLAINE: In that case, I'll have it. Take it up to my room, could you?

M. DE F.: On second thoughts, you can put it in my study and I'll have it in a minute.

MAID: Very good, monsieur.

(*She exits. Uneasy silence.*)

M. DE F. (*as controlled as he can manage*): Now, listen. I give you till ten o'clock tomorrow morning to have this . . . Rameau out of the house. And we'll say no more about it. Is that clear?

VERLAINE: Yes.

M. DE F.: Good.

VERLAINE: What if he refuses to go?

M. DE F.: Then I shall have him thrown out by the servants. And you after him.

VERLAINE: And my wife?

M. DE F.: Mathilde will of course stay here.

VERLAINE: On the contrary, Mathilde will of course come with me. Won't you Mathilde?

MATHILDE: No.

VERLAINE: If I say you will, you will.

MATHILDE: I won't.

MME M. DE F.: Stop it. There's absolutely no reason for either of you to leave. All you have to do, Paul, is to find somewhere else for M. Rimbaud to stay. Surely that shouldn't be impossible.

VERLAINE: I shall discuss the matter with him. (*Pause.*) I may invite him to stay another week.

M. DE F.: You'll do nothing of the sort. Tomorrow before ten o'clock or there'll be serious trouble. And another thing. You will kindly ask him to return all the objects he's pilfered before he leaves.

VERLAINE: What are you talking about?

M. DE F.: Just ask him, he'll know what I mean. (*To his wife.*) Are you coming dear? My coffee's getting cold. Mathilde?

MATHILDE: I'm going to my room.

VERLAINE: You're staying here. I want to talk to you.

M. DE F. Don't order her about like that, man.

VERLAINE: Why don't you mind your own business?

M. DE F.: You'd better be careful what you're saying.

MATHILDE (*tearfully*): I'm going to my room.

(*She exits in a rush. As she opens the door, we see that* RIMBAUD *is standing outside, listening, smiling dreamily. With a gesture of exquisite courtesy he steps back into the shadows to let* MATHILDE *pass. She stops dead for a moment, appalled by the apparition, and then hurries out.* M. DE F. *and* MME M. DE F. *have not seen* RIMBAUD, *who remains in the shadows.*)

M. DE F.: Now look what you've done. There's nothing more contemptible than a man who maltreats a woman.

VERLAINE: Unless it be a man who maltreats two.

(*They look at each other with hatred.*)

M. DE F.: Come on dear. Let's go.

MME M. DE F.: I think I'd better stay and have a word with Paul.

M. DE F.: Will you come with me!

(*Cowed by his tone,* MME M. DE F. *follows her husband through one door, as* RIMBAUD *enters by the other, still smiling.*)

RIMBAUD: Well. That was quite amusing.

VERLAINE: Were you listening?

RIMBAUD: Didn't miss a word.

VERLAINE: That man makes me furious. He's a caricature. I

frequently tell myself he can't possibly exist. But he does.

RIMBUAD: After a fashion.

(VERLAINE *grunts his agreement.*)

RIMBUAD: I think the moment may have come for me to leave.

VERLAINE: Why?

RIMBAUD: I feel I have outstayed my welcome.

VERLAINE: Look, if you think I'm going to let you be put out on the streets by that old sod. . . .

RIMBAUD: Yes?

VERLAINE: I'm not. It's outrageous.

RIMBAUD: It's his house.

VERLAINE: So it may be.

RIMBAUD: Then as I see it, you have two alternatives: either I go, or you make an issue of it and we both go.

VERLAINE: He wouldn't throw me out.

RIMBAUD: You know him better than I do.

VERLAINE: He would throw me out. He's been wanting to for months.

RIMBAUD: As I say then, you have two alternatives.

VERLAINE: Well . . . what do you think?

RIMBAUD: I think it's up to you.

VERLAINE (*stuttering indecisively*): I . . . well . . . look, why don't we discuss it over a few drinks? Then . . . er . . . I mean, look, go down and order one up for me, I want to have a word with Mathilde first, then I'll join you. Actually. . . .

RIMBAUD: What?

VERLAINE: Er, I don't see why you shouldn't move in with Cros for a bit, you see, Gill's away, and I was just thinking he'll have a spare bed. (*Pause. Then, sharply.*) What's so funny?

RIMBAUD: Nothing.

VERLAINE: Look, if you'd rather stay here, then. . . .

RIMBAUD: No, no. I'll go down and order you a drink. (*He goes over to the wall, takes a crucifix from it, and slips it in his pocket.*)

VERLAINE: What are you doing?

RIMBAUD: Stealing it. Crucifixes belong to the small category of things I can steal without it troubling my conscience in the

23

slightest. I always think one might as well make money out of God: he's not good for much else. (*Pause.*) Which reminds me, I've got a list here of the books I want from Mauté's library. I thought you might nick them for me, not all at once, one by one will do. They'll obviously be more use to me than they are to him. (*He hands* VERLAINE *the list.*) Don't be long, will you?

(*Exit* RIMBAUD. VERLAINE *looks after him, smiling. Then he turns, opens the door at the back of the stage, and calls upstairs.*)

VERLAINE: Mathilde! Mathilde!

(*While he is waiting,* VERLAINE *pours himself a drink and swallows it quickly. He looks nervous and uncomfortable. He pours another drink. Presently* MATHILDE *enters.*)

MATHILDE (*to break the silence*): I've just been into his room.

VERLAINE (*controlled*): Oh yes?

MATHILDE: It's disgusting. His bed's all filthy and open, and there are . . . animals crawling all over the pillow.

VERLAINE: Lice.

MATHILDE: What?

VERLAINE: Lice. He likes to keep a few handy so that if he meets a priest in the street, he's always got something appropriate to throw at him.

MATHILDE: I don't understand.

VERLAINE: Never mind. (*Pause.*) Anyway, what were you doing in his room?

MATHILDE: I went in to see if he'd returned our crucifix.

VERLAINE: And?

MATHILDE: He hasn't. He's stolen it.

VERLAINE: I see.

MATHILDE: Well, you're to make him give it back.

VERLAINE (*speaking very distinctly*): He's left the house.

MATHILDE: You must get it back from him.

VERLAINE: I have no intention of doing anything of the sort. If your father wants it back he can go and look for it himself. As far as I'm concerned, if he's capable of throwing that boy out on to the streets without a penny, he deserves to lose more than a few religious knick-knacks. He's got no

24

right to have Christ hanging all over his walls. You people don't understand what poverty is. Do you realize that in Charleville, when Rimbaud wanted a book, he had to go and steal it off the bookstall?

MATHILDE: That proves what sort of a person he is.

(VERLAINE *punches* MATHILDE *hard in the face. She topples over, bringing down a small table with a resounding crash. There is a brief silence.* MATHILDE *moans softly.* VERLAINE *starts forward, and helps her off the floor.*)

VERLAINE: I'm sorry . . . I'm sorry . . . dear . . . sorry . . . I couldn't help it. You shouldn't have said that. I'm very . . . I've never been so humiliated as I was just now when Rimbaud left. We'll have to . . . when you've had the baby, we'll get out of here and things will be much easier.

(MATHILDE *is weeping soundlessly.* VERLAINE *waits for her to say something, but she remains silent.*)

It'll be different once we get away from your bloody father.

(*Enter* M. DE F. *and* MME M. DE F.)

M. DE F.: What's going on? (*Silence.*) Mm?

MATHILDE: Nothing.

M. DE F.: What was all that noise then?

MATHILDE: I . . . knocked the table over.

MME M. DE F.: Are you all right dear?

(MATHILDE *nods, very pale.*)

M. DE F.: Well, have you spoken to that fellow yet?

VERLAINE (*savagely*): Yes.

(*He strides over to the door and exits. A quick black-out, as* M. DE F. *looks after him, surprised.*)

CURTAIN

Scene 3

Charles Cros' apartment; 5th November, 1871.
A modest but tastefully furnished room. There are numerous books

and papers lying about. On the walls, drawings, caricatures and photographs. When the curtain goes up, RIMBAUD *is lying on a divan and* VERLAINE *is sitting in an armchair.*

VERLAINE: You see, I didn't think it really mattered who I married. I thought anybody would do. Anybody within reason.

RIMBAUD: I don't know why you wanted to get married in the first place.

VERLAINE: I was tired of it all. I was living with Mother then. Only because I was too lazy to live by myself and look after myself. She did everything—and to an extent it was all right. I did what I liked and only went home to sleep or to eat or to change. But in the end it began to wear me down, the office was so boring and home was so boring, and I started to drink more and more and I had to keep slipping off to the brothel, things got worse and worse. Day after day I'd wake up fully clothed, covered with mud or with all the skin off my knuckles, feeling sick and nursing a dim memory of $3\frac{1}{2}$ minutes with some horrible tart who hadn't even bothered to take her shoes off.

This can't go on, I said.

It has to stop.

One day I went round to see Sivry, who was doing the music for a farce I was going to write and as he was showing me up to his room we passed through the Mautés' main room, you know, and there she was, standing with her back to us, looking out of the window. I think we startled her because she turned round very quickly. I was stunned, she was so beautiful. She was wearing a grey and green dress and she stood in the window with the sun going down behind her. Sivry said, had I met his half-sister, Mathilde, and I said, no, unfortunately I hadn't. So he introduced me and said I was a poet and she smiled and said how nice, she was very fond of poets.

I tell you, that was it.

A week later, I was in Arras, I woke up in bed with the most grisly scrubber you can imagine, sweaty she was, snoring. I was trying to tiptoe away when she woke up and called me back.

I went back.

Later on that morning I wrote to Sivry and told him I wanted to marry Mathilde.

I thought she was ideal. Plenty of money. Well enough brought up to have all the wifely virtues. Innocent. Beautiful. Sixteen. She would look after me. And be there every night in my bed.

I had to wait over a year before I could have her. It was agony. Delicious. I used to go there every evening and look at her. When the wedding was put off for the third time, I practically went berserk. And when it finally took place, I couldn't believe it. I felt giddy all day. The day seemed to last for weeks; but the night was short enough.

The next few months were marvellous, you know. I didn't care about the war, the Prussians could do what they liked as far as I was concerned. I was otherwise engaged. I can't tell you how wonderful it was. It was like Valmont and Cécile. It was a kind of legalized corruption. She was impossibly coy at first, she didn't like it, she didn't understand it, it hurt. And then slowly she began to take to it, she relaxed, she became . . . inventive. And then one night, when I was very tired, she suggested it.

(*Silence.*)

RIMBAUD: And now you have a son.

VERLAINE: And now I have a son.

(*Silence.*)

RIMBAUD: What happened last night, anyway?

VERLAINE: Well, I . . . can't remember it very clearly. As you know I wasn't quite myself when I left you last night. My idea was to go to bed with her, as I think I mentioned to you.

RIMBAUD: Many times.

VERLAINE: Yes, well I thought, it's a week since the child was born, it ought to be all right by now. I said I'd be careful, but, I mean, it's been such a long time. Anyway, it was no good, she wouldn't.

27

RIMBAUD: So what happened?

VERLAINE: I don't know, God knows.

RIMBAUD: Did you hit her again?

VERLAINE: No, no, not this time. I woke up, as in Arras, with my boots on the pillow, and tiptoed away. But she didn't call me back.

RIMBAUD: So you're still frustrated?

(VERLAINE *nods. Silence.*)

RIMBAUD: Why don't you leave her?

VERLAINE: What?

RIMBAUD: Leave her.

VERLAINE: Why?

RIMBAUD: Because she's no good to you.

VERLAINE: What do you mean?

RIMBAUD: Do you love her?

VERLAINE: Yes, I suppose so.

RIMBAUD: Have you got anything in common with her?

VERLAINE: No.

RIMBAUD: Is she intelligent?

VERLAINE: No.

RIMBAUD: Does she understand you?

VERLAINE: No.

RIMBAUD: So the only thing she can give you is sex?

VERLAINE! Well. . . .

RIMBAUD: Can't you find anyone else?

VERLAINE: I. . . .

RIMBAUD: You're not that fussy, are you?

VERLAINE: No.

RIMBAUD: Anyone within reason would do, wouldn't they?

VERLAINE: Within reason.

RIMBAUD: What about me?

(*Silence.* RIMBAUD *laughs.*)

RIMBAUD: Are you a poet?

(*Silence.* VERLAINE *smiles uneasily.*)

VERLAINE (*cautiously*): Yes.

RIMBAUD: I'd say not.

VERLAINE: Why?

RIMBAUD: Well, I hope you wouldn't describe that last volume of pre-marital junk as poetry?

VERLAINE: I most certainly would. Very beautiful love poetry, that is.

RIMBAUD: But you've just admitted that all you wanted to do was to go to bed with her.

VERLAINE: That doesn't make the poems any less beautiful.

RIMBAUD: Doesn't it? Doesn't it matter that they're lies?

VERLAINE: They're not lies. I love her.

RIMBAUD: Love?

VERLAINE: Yes.

RIMBAUD: No such thing.

VERLAINE: What do you mean?

RIMBAUD: I mean it doesn't exist. Self-interest exists. Attachment based on personal gain exists. Complacency exists. But not love.

VERLAINE: You're wrong.

RIMBAUD: Well, all right, if you care to describe what binds families and married couples together as love rather than stupidity or selfishness or fear, then we'll say that love does exist. In which case it's useless, it doesn't help. It's the invention of cowards.

VERLAINE: You're wrong.

(*Silence.*)

RIMBAUD: I have sometimes felt tempted to take my knife and kill a beautiful girl rather elaborately in public. But Judge, I would say, it's what you people do so tastefully and respectably every day. I admit mine was a little messy, but I'm only a beginner, your honour. Am I right in thinking, my lord, that I'm not on trial for emulating my betters, but for doing it in such a personally amusing way? But the judge would only smile benevolently and say, of course not my son, your approach may have been a trifle muddle-headed, but we approve of your commendable intentions. However, I'm sure you'll appreciate the principles involved, if, for the further entertainment of the general public, I sentence you to be guillotined.

(VERLAINE *is pleased with this. Silence.*)

VERLAINE: You still haven't told me why I should leave my

29

wife.

RIMBAUD: When I was in Paris in February this year, when everything was in a state of chaos, I was staying the night in a barracks and I was sexually assaulted by four drunken soldiers. It wasn't a particularly agreeable experience, but when I got back to Charleville, thinking about it, I began to realize how valuable it had been to me. It clarified things in my mind which had been vague. It gave my imagination textures. And I understood that what I needed, to be the first poet of this century, the first poet since Racine or since the Greeks, was to experience everything in my body. I knew what it was like to be a model pupil, top of the class, now I wanted to disgust them instead of pleasing them. I knew what it was like to take communion, I wanted to take drugs. I knew what it was like to be chaste, I wanted perversions. It was no longer enough for me to be one person, I decided to be everyone. I decided to be a genius. I decided to be Christ. I decided to originate the future.

The fact that I often regarded my ambition as ludicrous and pathetic pleased me, it was what I wanted, contrast, conflict inside my head, that was good. While other writers looked at themselves in the mirror, accepted what they saw, and jotted it down, I liked to see a mirror in the mirror, so that I could turn round whenever I felt like it and always find endless vistas of myself.

However, what I say is immaterial, it's what I write that counts.

If you help me, I'll help you.

VERLAINE: How can I help you?

RIMBAUD: By leaving your wife. As far as I can see, it's the only hope there is for you. Not only are you unhappy as you are, it's not even doing you any good. What are you going to do, write domestic poetry for the rest of your life? Bringing up baby? Epics of the Civil Service? Or will you be forced, you, Verlaine, to write impersonal poetry? Foolish plays and feeble historical reconstructions? If you leave her and come with me, both of us will benefit. And when we've got as much from one another as we can, we split up and

30

move on. You could even go back to your wife again.

It's just a suggestion, it's up to you.

Anyway, I certainly won't be allowed to stay here much longer.

VERLAINE: What makes you think that?

RIMBAUD: Instinct. Come with me when I leave.

VERLAINE: You seem to forget that I have a son now.

RIMBAUD: On the contrary, that's what makes it so ideal. If you leave your wife now, you won't be leaving her alone. She can spend all her time bringing up her son. That's what my father did, he just upped and left us one day, he couldn't have done a wiser thing. Except he'd left it a bit late.

VERLAINE: But how would we live?

RIMBAUD: You've got some money, haven't you?

VERLAINE: Ah, now I understand. I help you by supporting you, and you help me by renewing my rusty old inspiration. Is that it?

RIMBAUD: Not altogether.

VERLAINE: Well, how else are you going to help me, then?

RIMBAUD: You name it.

(They look at each other for a moment, sparring. Then CROS enters, talking. With him are ÉTIENNE CARJAT, 43, neatly and soberly dressed, and ERNEST CABANER, 38, a tall cadaverous, bearded man, wearing a tattered, flowing orange cloak.)

CROS: . . . it could be used for music, as well, you see.

(General salutations.)

CROS: Rimbaud, this is Étienne Carjat, a photographer, and this is Ernest Cabaner, one of the four musicians of the Apocalypse.

VERLAINE: Known to his friends as Jesus Christ. After three years' absinthe.

CABANER: It's the p-profile, you see.

CARJAT *(to CROS)*: Anyway, go on.

CROS: What about?

CARJAT: About the paleophone.

CROS: Well, that's about it, really, I mean, it's very much like photography. Only instead of photographing a man's face, you photograph his voice. Then, twenty years later, just as

31

you might open the photograph album, you simply put the relevant cylinder into the paleophone and listen to him reading his poem or singing his song.

CARJAT: And you think you could invent a machine like that which worked?

CROS: Yes. Perfectly possible.

RIMBAUD (*sarcastically*): Like your scheme for communicating with the inhabitants of Mars.

CROS: Yes.

VERLAINE: Well, why don't you do it, then? Why don't you ever do anything about it?

CROS: I don't know. I can't be bothered with all the organization and effort.

VERLAINE: You're an idle bugger.

CROS (*mock dignity*): I'm a man of ideas.

CARJAT: Well, you should do something about this one. It could make you a fortune.

CROS: Maybe I will.

VERLAINE: Haven't seen you for a long time, Cabaner.

CABANER: No, I've been avoiding going out recently.

VERLAINE: Why?

CABANER: Well . . . I always get lost. (*The laughter of the others makes him a little indignant.*) Anyway, I've been engaged on a m-major work.

CARJAT: What?

CABANER: A cantata. A work of epic scale and breathtaking majesty.

VERLAINE: On what theme?

CABANER: It's about a meat pie.

RIMBAUD (*pleased by this*): I thought cantatas were supposed to be about God.

CABANER: They can be about what you like. I don't like God. I like meat pies. There have been thousands of cantatas about the glory of God, but never, never one about the glory of meat pies.

CROS: How's it going?

CABANER: Well. Very well. I have written the most m-magnificent fugal chorale to open the work. It's too complex to sing to you, and anyway I've forgotten the tune.

RIMBAUD: Do you remember the words?

CABANER: Yes:

"Go tell the cook that I love her,
Go tell the cook that I care,
Her wondrous and exquisite meat pies,
Have filled me with hope and despair."

RIMBAUD (*smiling*): Excellent.

(CARJAT, *unamused, leans forward to address* RIMBAUD.)

CARJAT: How would you like to be photographed?

RIMBAUD: Not particularly.

CARJAT: Because I'd like to photograph you. I find your appearance very striking. You have a very fine bone structure.

RIMBAUD: Really?

CARJAT: Yes. I don't think much of your poetry, but I love your bone structure.

RIMBAUD: Why don't you think much to my poetry?

CARJAT: Well, actually I think it's very promising. But it seems to me that all that ingenuity is rather marred by . . . well, not exactly a juvenile urge to shock, but something of the sort.

RIMBAUD: And were you shocked when you read it?

CARJAT: No, I . . . no, of course not.

RIMBAUD: Then why should you suppose that I intended you to be?

CARJAT: Well . . . that's not really the point.

VERLAINE: Seems fair enough to me.

CARJAT: I . . . I could object to your technical approach.

RIMBAUD: I could object to your tie.

CARJAT: Well, if you're going to take that attitude. . . .

CROS: He doesn't like discussing his poetry.

CARJAT: I see.

(*Uneasy silence.*)

CABANER: Did I hear someone say something about going for a drink?

VERLAINE: I think someone may have mentioned it.

(VERLAINE *and* CABANER *rise.*)

CARJAT: Ah, look, just a minute. (*To* CROS.) Are you going to show me that thing before we go?

CROS: Oh yes, of course. (*He rummages around for a moment.*) If I can find it. (*To* RIMBAUD.) Have you seen that display copy of *The Artist* for May? The one with my poems in it.

RIMBAUD: Er . . . I seem to remember seeing it. Not in here, though.

CROS: Funny. Look, I won't be a minute. It can't be far away. (*Exit* CROS.)

CABANER: Hurry up, I'm thirsty.

RIMBAUD (*urgently*): Where do you live, M. Cabaner?

CABANER: W-where do I live? (*Pause.*) Where *do* I live?

VERLAINE: At the Hotel des Étrangers.

RIMBAUD: Where is that?

CABANER: Oh, it's a big place. The road, as I remember, is n-named after some great writer.

VERLAINE: Racine.

CABANER: That's the boy.

RIMBAUD: And do you have a lot of room there?

CABANER: Yes. Oh, yes, I have an enormous s-studio.

RIMBAUD: Could you put me up?

CABANER: Yes.

RIMBAUD: Tonight?

CABANER (*puzzled*): Y-yes.

RIMBAUD: Good. Lovely. See you later.

(*Suddenly a great roar from* CROS *offstage.*)

RIMBAUD: Tell Cros I had to use something. (*He moves over to the door.*) They were lousy poems anyway.

(*Exit* RIMBAUD. *A moment later,* CROS *storms in, holding a once-glossy and handsome magazine, with several pages torn out.*)

CROS: Look. Look at it. All my poems have been torn out. I found it in the lavatory.

CABANER (*concentrating on remembering the message*): He, er, the young man s-said he had to use something.

CROS (*incensed*): He said *what?*

Scene 4

The Café du Théâtre du Bobino; 20th December, 1871.
A dinner of the Vilains Bonshommes, a poetry society. Among the
guests VERLAINE, RIMBAUD, CROS, CARJAT *and* CABANER. *Clothes*
ranging from the impeccable to the scruffy (VERLAINE, RIMBAUD,
CABANER). *Everyone is seated, except for* JEAN AICARD, *a respectable*
and portly poet, who is in the middle of a reading of some of his
poems. VERLAINE *looks bored and drunk,* RIMBAUD *disgusted. As the*
curtain rises, there is a polite ripple of applause from AICARD'*s*
audience.

AICARD: Thank you. I should like to end by. . . .
    (*He pauses as* RIMBAUD *breaks into boisterous applause.*)
    . . . by reading a poem from a collection I am planning for
    children. I would ask you to bear in mind that the poem is
    written expressly for children, although as with all worth-
    while work for children, it is hoped that what is said is not
    entirely without relevance to adults. The poem is called
    "Green Absinthe".
    (*He clears his throat.* RIMBAUD *belches.*)
    "Green Absinthe."
    "Green absinthe is the potion of the damned. . . ."
    (RIMBAUD *splutters.*)
    "A deadly poison silting up the veins,
    While wife and child sit weeping in their slum. . . ."
RIMBAUD (*distinctly*): I don't believe it.
    (*A certain sensation.* AICARD *soldiers on.*)
AICARD: "The drunkard pours absinthe into his brains."
RIMBAUD: Shit.
AICARD: "Oh! Drunkard, most contemptible of men. . . ."
RIMBAUD: Shit.
AICARD (*his voice cracking*): "Degraded, fallen, sinful and
    obtuse. . . ."
RIMBAUD (*delighted*): It is! It is! Authentic shit!

AICARD: "Degraded, fallen, sinful and obtuse. . . ."

RIMBAUD: I like it.

AICARD (*doggedly*): "Degraded, fallen, sinful and obtuse
You scruple not to beat your wife and child. . . ."

RIMBAUD: For trying to deprive you of the juice.

(*Pandemonium. Protests, laughter, shouting.* AICARD *subsides
weakly, then gets up again.* CARJAT *springs to his feet.*)

CARJAT: Get out, you!

(*Silence falls.*)

RIMBAUD: Me?

CARJAT: Yes you, you offensive little bastard. Get out, or I'll
throw you out. Who the hell do you think you are?

RIMBAUD: I think I may, may I not, be permitted to raise some
objection against the butchering of French poetry?

CARJAT: No. You may not. Now apologize and get out.

(*He moves towards* RIMBAUD, *who rises and grips*
VERLAINE'*s sword-stick.*)

VERLAINE: Careful.

RIMBAUD (*to* CARJAT. *Grim and pale*): Don't come any nearer.

CARJAT: If you think you can frighten me with that thing. . . .

(RIMBAUD *draws the sword.*)

(*ends weakly*): . . . you've got another think coming.

RIMBAUD (*almost a whisper*): Don't come any nearer.

(*Deadlock. They watch each other venomously. Then* CARJAT
attacks, and RIMBAUD *slashes out at him.* CARJAT *stops,
appalled, cries out, grasps his wrist. Blood flows. Chaos.*)

VERLAINE: Careful, I said.

RIMBAUD (*turning to Aicard, with a great roar*): And now, you.

(*He tears down on* AICARD, *who, for a moment is transfixed
with horror, before breaking and running for his life.*)
Miserable poetaster!

(*He pursues* AICARD *round the room, slashing wildly at him.
Finally* AICARD *gets the table between himself and* RIMBAUD.
Meanwhile RIMBAUD *is resisting all attempts to disarm him
by laying about him at anyone who comes too close.*)
In the days of François Premier, wise and benevolent giants
roamed the countryside. And one, let me tell you, one of
their . . . natural functions was to rid the world of pedants,

fools and writers of no talent . . . (*he leaps up on to the table*) by . . . by pissing on them from a great height, and . . . and. . . .

(*At this point he passes out, crashing spectacularly to the ground.* VERLAINE *and* CROS *seize him and hurry out with him amid general confusion.*)

CURTAIN

Scene 5

The Café du Rat Mort; 29th June, 1872.

The café is fairly empty. VERLAINE *and* RIMBAUD *sit at a table, drinking absinthe. Throughout the scene,* RIMBAUD's *behaviour is curious and distant, as if he has been taking hashish or drinking all night. Occasionally he shakes off this air of drugged or drunken fatigue for a time, only to relapse into dreamy contemplation when, for instance,* VERLAINE *speaks at any length.*

RIMBAUD : The first thing he did, it seems, when he was given the ring, a magic ring you understand, was to summon up a beautiful woman, the most beautiful he could imagine. And they were wonderfully happy and lived alone on a light blue southern island. Then one day he explained to her that with the ring he could grant her anything she wanted, and she asked him to build her a city. So he caused a city to grow up out of the sea, full of churches and echoing courtyards, and quite empty. She was so delighted with it that he granted her another wish, and she asked for a ship. So he gave her a magnificent galleon which needed no crew to look after the silk hangings and golden figurehead. It seemed to give her such happiness that he decided to grant her one more wish. "One more wish," he said. "I will grant you one more wish."

"Give me the ring," she said.

He gave it to her. She smiled serenely at him and threw

37

it into the sea. At once she disappeared, the ship disappeared, and the city slowly sank back under the water.

For a long time after that the man sat looking out to sea without moving. Finally he began to weep because he understood what he had done and knew that now it was all over, and that he would be alone for ever.

That was it. Something like that.

Colour is what's missing, colour. That's what this gives you, thick colours you can smell and hear. Otherwise everything is grey and dull. I want to go somewhere I can get it without this. South. Away from the dusty mantelpiece of Europe. If I may so express myself. (*He chuckles.*)

Let's leave. I've always wanted to see the sea. We can't possibly go on as we are. Can we? I mean. . . . I mean, let's leave.

God, my hands are cold.

Can't we leave?

VERLAINE: Here?

RIMBAUD: Paris, Paris.

VERLAINE: Well. . . .

RIMBAUD: We certainly can't go on as we are. It's been dragging on for months as it is. You can't keep sending me home whenever she threatens a divorce and summoning me back when the coast looks clear. What's needed, if . . . (*he blinks, concentrates*) if I may use a crude term I know you find distasteful, is a decision.

VERLAINE: Ah, decisions. . . .

RIMBAUD: Yes.

VERLAINE: I always say, show me a decisive man and I'll show you a fool.

RIMBAUD: Wishful thinking.

VERLAINE: Anyway, she's not very well at the moment.

RIMBAUD: I'm not surprised, if you keep setting fire to her.

VERLAINE (*indignantly*): I haven't set fire to her since May.

(*They both laugh.*)

VERLAINE: It's not very funny.

(*They both laugh some more.*)

RIMBAUD: It's pathetic. (*He stops laughing, abruptly.*) Pathetic,

Your acts of violence are always curiously disgusting.

VERLAINE: What do you mean?

RIMBAUD: They're not clean. You're always in a drunken stupor when you commit them. You beat up Mathilde, or hit me, or throw your son against the wall—and then you start apologizing and grovelling.

VERLAINE: I don't like hurting people.

RIMBAUD: Then don't. And if you do, do it coolly, and don't insult your victim by feeling sorry for him afterwards. (*Silence.*)

VERLAINE: I don't think I ever told you about the most terrible of my little tantrums—when I attacked my brother and sisters.

RIMBAUD: I didn't think you had any.

VERLAINE: Oh, yes. Like you, I have one brother and two sisters. The difference between mine and yours is that mine are dead.

My mother had three miscarriages before I was born— and being of a rather morbid turn of mind, she kept the results in a cupboard in the bedroom, preserved, ominously enough, in alcohol. There they were, Nicolas, Stéphanie, and Élisa, stacked away on the top shelf in three enormous jars. I'll never forget the first time I came across them, when I was a small boy. I was fooling around in the bedroom, burrowing in the cupboard, which I'd never dared do before, when I saw these great jars. The light was pretty bad and I couldn't make out what was in them at first, so I got a chair and stood on it. It was one of the most revolting moments of my life. I suddenly saw these three little puckered people, lined up, staring at me in a strangely knowing way.

I had no idea what they were. I dimly associated them with preserved plums, and for weeks after that my stomach turned over whenever we had roast.

When I found out they were my own flesh and blood, they assumed a monumental importance in my life. I used to watch Mother dusting them every Thursday, and consult them on all matters of moment. Not that they were very helpful. They remained expressionless and inscrutable at all times, and as the years wore on, I began to detect a certain superciliousness in their attitude, a kind of amused contempt for their younger brother, which came to be very wounding.

The older I got, the more I resented them.

They had a right to be complacent, I thought, because they'd had it very easy and didn't know any better. But they had no right to despise me for being less fortunate than they were. When Mother told me how difficult and dangerous my birth had been, I often felt there had been some terrible mistake and that my place was up there with them in a large glass jar, meditating quietly and being dusted on Thursdays. "If any of you have lived," I used to tell them, "I wouldn't have had to. So it's all your fault." They looked back at me, smug, sceptical and unblinking. And I envied their peace.

One night only a couple of years ago, I got very drunk indeed. I was really at the bottom of the pit, things couldn't have been blacker. As happens from time to time, I had a nasty attack of the vomits, racking out blood and bits and all the accumulated muck I'd been pouring into myself for years, I wished I was dead, you know how it is, the worst. That's when I get violent. When I see things as they really are.

I went to the cupboard and looked at Nicolas, Stéphanie and Élisa, sitting there comfortably, wise and gloating. And lifted my stick and smashed the jars.

(*Silence.*)

RIMBAUD: And?

VERLAINE: I remember being saturated in alcohol—and a glimpse of them grotesquely marooned in their broken jars before I passed out. The next day when I looked, they were back, just as before, in identical jars, and Mother never said a word about it. Were it not for the fact that I surprised a look of active dislike on their faces when I next visited them, I'd be inclined to write off the whole incident as a ghastly dream.

RIMBAUD: Few corpses can have led such eventful lives.

(VERLAINE *laughs, summons the waiter.*)

VERLAINE: Two.

(*Silence.*)

RIMBAUD: You have digressed. Strayed from the point.

VERLAINE: We have all day and all night to get back to it. Whatever it was. Is.

RIMBAUD: It's time to leave.

VERLAINE: I've just ordered another drink.

RIMBAUD: Paris.

VERLAINE: Oh.

RIMBAUD: This is the time to go, the summer. We will be children of the sun and live in pagan pleasure. (*He smiles.*) The happiest times of my life were when I ran away from home. Walking through fields in the sun, or sheltering from a shower in a wood, sleeping under hedges, ham sandwich and a beer for supper, I just carried on until I had no money left, and even then it didn't seem to matter. I've never known such long and coloured days. Only I never got far enough. I wanted to follow a river to the sea, or walk to Africa and cross a desert. I wanted heat and violence of landscape.

But what I didn't have on those days often added to their harmony.

VERLAINE (*a trace of irony*): It sounds idyllic.

RIMBAUD: It was. Much more idyllic than that filthy little room where I sleep when you're making love to Mathilde, and don't sleep when you're making love to me.

VERLAINE: You do sleep. I often watch you sleeping.

RIMBAUD: You often wake me up. (*Pause.*) Isn't it time you left Mathilde?

VERLAINE: Why? I love her.

RIMBAUD: You can't possibly.

VERLAINE: I love her body.

RIMBAUD: There are other bodies.

VERLAINE: That's not the point. I love Mathilde's body.

RIMBAUD: But not her soul?

VERLAINE: I think it's less important to love the soul than to love the body. After all, the soul may be immortal, we have

41

plenty of time for the soul: but flesh rots.

(RIMBAUD *laughs*.)

VERLAINE: Do you find that amusing?

RIMBAUD: Not really.

VERLAINE: If people laugh at flesh it is because they do not love its textures, or its shape and smell, as I do. Or its sadness.

RIMBAUD (*coldly*): Quite possibly.

VERLAINE: It is my love of flesh which makes me faithful.

RIMBAUD: Faithful? What do you mean?

VERLAINE: It's possible to be faithful to more than one person. I'm faithful to all my lovers, because once I love them, I will always love them. And when I am alone in the evening or the early morning, I close my eyes and celebrate them all, and see the perfection of their bodies moving and coiling in limitless and supple patterns. They all leave images which I am faithful to.

RIMBAUD: That's not faithfulness, it's nostalgia. If you don't want to leave Mathilde, it's not because you're faithful, it's because you're weak.

VERLAINE: If strength involves brutality, I prefer to be weak.

RIMBAUD: With you, weakness involves brutality as well. (*Pause*.) Don't expect me to be faithful to you.

VERLAINE: I don't.

(*Silence*.)

RIMBAUD: I'm leaving Paris next week. You can come with me or not, as you like.

VERLAINE: Where are you going?

RIMBAUD: I don't know. Just away. Are you coming?

VERLAINE: I. . . .

RIMBAUD: Or are you staying with Mathilde?

VERLAINE: I don't know. The thought of losing either of you is unbearable. I don't know. Why are you so harsh with me?

RIMBAUD: Because you need it.

VERLAINE: Why? Isn't it enough for you to know that I love you more than I've ever loved anyone, and that I always will love you?

RIMBAUD: Shut up, you snivelling drunk.

VERLAINE: Tell me if you love me.

RIMBAUD: Oh, for God's sake. . . .

VERLAINE: Please.

(*Silence.*)

Please. It's important to me.

RIMBAUD: Why?

VERLAINE: Please.

(*Silence.*)

RIMBAUD: I . . . you know I'm very fond of you . . . we've been very happy sometimes . . . I. . . .

(*A very long silence.* RIMBAUD *blushes deeply. He produces a large knife from his pocket, and picks at the table with it.*)

(*Almost inaudibly*): Do you love me?

VERLAINE: What?

RIMBAUD: Do you love me?

VERLAINE (*puzzled*): Yes.

RIMBAUD: Then put your hands on the table.

VERLAINE: What?

RIMBAUD: Put your hands on the table.

(VERLAINE *does so.*)

Palm upwards.

(VERLAINE *turns his hands palm upwards.* RIMBAUD *looks at them for a moment, and then with short. brutal hacks, stabs at both of them.* VERLAINE *sits looking at his hands in amazement, as blood begins to drip down on to the floor.*)

The only unbearable thing is that nothing is unbearable.

(VERLAINE *stares uncomprehendingly at him, then gets up and stumbles out of the café.* RIMBAUD *watches him leave, then gets up himself and hurries out after him.*)

CURTAIN

Scene 6

A hotel room in Brussels; 22nd July, 1872.

VERLAINE *is lying half-in and half-on the rumpled bed.* MATHILDE *stands with her back to the audience, getting dressed.*

43

VERLAINE: That was wonderful, darling.

(*Silence.*)

VERLAINE: Wonderful.

MATHILDE: Can you pass me my stockings? (*She indicates the chair by the bed, where they are neatly arranged.*)

VERLAINE: Why don't you come and lie down and relax for a bit? You don't have to get dressed right away, do you?

MATHILDE: It's getting late.

VERLAINE: Nonsense, it's only about half-past eight.

MATHILDE: Someone might come.

VERLAINE: Who?

MATHILDE: Mummy.

VERLAINE: I thought you weren't meeting her till lunch. Anyway, we're married aren't we, for God's sake?

(MATHILDE *walks over to the chair, picks up her stockings, sits down on the bed, and starts to put them on.*)

Do you remember . . .

(*He leans forward and strokes her hair, then turns her face to him and kisses her. She submits briefly, and, it seems, without enthusiasm to his embrace.*)

. . . happier times?

MATHILDE: Yes. (*She continues dressing.*) Are you coming back to Paris with me?

VERLAINE: I . . . don't know.

MATHILDE: Why don't you want to?

VERLAINE: I do want to, it's just . . . it's just I don't think it's safe in Paris any more. I mean . . . I mean they're still arresting people connected with the Commune. Look what happened to Sivry. Four months in jail for practically no reason at all. And who gave him his job? I did. I had a very important job, you know. I was virtually in charge of the propaganda press.

MATHILDE: I know, but that was over a year ago.

VERLAINE: The police are slow, but methodical. They don't forgive and forget. I couldn't stand going to jail. (*Pause.*) That's why I think it's better if I play it safe and stay out of the country for a few months.

MATHILDE: With Rimbaud.

44

VERLAINE: Well. . . .

MATHILDE: I suppose he's wanted by the police too.

VERLAINE: Er. . . .

MATHILDE: Why don't you want to come back?

VERLAINE: I. . . .

MATHILDE: Why do you prefer him to me?

VERLAINE: I don't, love, I don't. (*Pause.*) It's just . . . I'll tell you what it is. I can't stand living with your parents any more. I will not be pushed around by that stupid old man. I refuse to put up with his gruesome middle-aged omniscience and the aggressive pride he takes in his own uselessness. I can't understand what makes you want to stay there.

MATHILDE: Because . . . because it's not safe anywhere else.

VERLAINE: What do you mean?

MATHILDE: You know what I mean.

(*Silence.*)

VERLAINE: It's only when I've been drinking, dear. It's only when I'm drunk, and it all becomes too much for me. It's only when things are impossible. You know I don't mean it.

MATHILDE: At the time you mean it.

(*Silence.*)

MATHILDE: You know . . . you know Daddy wants me to get a divorce?

VERLAINE: I've told you before. . . .

MATHILDE: He says if you go away with Rimbaud, you're deserting me and I can get a divorce. He says. . . .

VERLAINE (*shouting*): It's nothing to do with him. It's me you're married to, not him. (*More calmly.*) Do you want a divorce?

MATHILDE: No. (*She begins to cry soundlessly, her body shaking with sobs.*)

VERLAINE: Don't cry, love. (*He puts his arms round her, and soothes her.*) That's better.

MATHILDE: Are you going to come with me?

VERLAINE. I don't know, love, I. . . .

MATHILDE: Not home, I don't mean home, I mean abroad.

VERLAINE: Abroad?

MATHILDE: Yes, I had this idea, I thought of this idea, don't be

45

angry. I thought we might . . . emigrate. To Canada.

VERLAINE: Canada?

MATHILDE: New Caledonia. There are quite a lot of our friends out there, you know, Rochefort and . . . and Louise Michel.

VERLAINE: Is she?

MATHILDE: Yes.

VERLAINE: Louise Michel, the red virgin?

MATHILDE: Yes, and I thought . . . I thought, as you said you wanted to write a book about the Commune, they'd be able to help. And . . . I've heard it's lovely out there, the country, and the forests, and we could try again.

VERLAINE: What about the baby?

MATHILDE: Well, that's up to you, but I thought, if you wanted to that is, we could leave him behind, I mean, Mummy would be only too pleased to look after him for a couple of years, or however long . . . we wanted to stay.

VERLAINE: It's a nice idea. . . .

MATHILDE: It's the best thing we could do, Paul. You could write, and be quiet, and . . . and it'd be like it was when we were first married, and. . . .

VERLAINE: What?

MATHILDE: Doesn't matter.

VERLAINE: No, go on.

MATHILDE: Well, I . . . was only going to say you could stop . . . it would be easy for you . . . if you wanted to . . . stop drinking.

VERLAINE: You're frightened of me, aren't you?

(MATHILDE *doesn't answer*, VERLAINE *puts his arms round her again.*)

I do love you, you know. (*He kisses her.*) Don't think I like getting drunk. I mean I do like getting drunk, but I don't like being drunk. Or anyway . . . when I hit you or . . . do any of the things I do, I feel so terrible about it the next day, the only thing I can think of is to get drunk again and forget about it. I can't stop, I can never stop, there's no end to it. I'm not angry with you, when you mention it. Most of the time I want to give it up as much as you want

46

me to. But it's as difficult as deciding to wake up when you're asleep.

Perhaps I could wake up in Canada, because it's clean there, and fresh, and hard. That's what I want most, you know, it's what I really want most, I want to live quietly, and work hard and well, and make love to you, and have children, would that be possible do you think? It should be easy, do you think it's possible?

MATHILDE: Yes, it's possible.

VERLAINE: Can you see us, can you see us living in a log cabin, or whatever they have? Writing all day and then reading my work to you in the evening as we watch the sun set into the Pacific. Would it be like that?

MATHILDE: It might be.

VERLAINE: Then let's go, for Christ's sake, let's go. Before it's too late.

MATHILDE: We can go whenever you like.

VERLAINE: God, I love you.

(*He kisses her again, a long, clinging kiss, at the end of which he begins to undress her. She pulls away from him.*)

MATHILDE: No, not now.

VERLAINE: Why not?

(*She doesn't answer, attending to her clothes.* VERLAINE *sits up and touches her shoulder.*)

VERLAINE: Come on.

MATHILDE: No.

VERLAINE: Why not?

MATHILDE: I'm very tired. I've been in the train all night and I didn't sleep very well.

VERLAINE: Please.

MATHILDE: Look, I'm supposed to be meeting Mummy for breakfast, and I'm late already. Why don't you get dressed and come with me?

VERLAINE: I don't want breakfast, I want you.

MATHILDE: There'll be other times.

VERLAINE: Will there?

MATHILDE: Well, of course. Help me with this, will you?

(VERLAINE *helps her into her stern, billowing dress.*)

47

VERLAINE: What's this meeting Mummy for breakfast?

MATHILDE: I promised to. I think she hopes you'll come too.

VERLAINE: Tell her I don't feel like breakfast today.

MATHILDE: Can I tell her it's all right about Canada?

VERLAINE: What?

MATHILDE: Canada.

VERLAINE: What's it got to do with her?

MATHILDE: Well, she's got to be told, hasn't she?

VERLAINE: Now?

MATHILDE: Well, it *is* all right, isn't it?

VERLAINE: I . . . don't know.

MATHILDE: But, you just said. . . .

VERLAINE: I know, I know what I said.
   (*Silence.*)

MATHILDE: If it's money you're worrying about, Daddy's already
   said he'll pay the fare. . . . (*She stops dead, realizing that
   she has made a bad mistake.*)

VERLAINE: What?

MATHILDE: Nothing.

VERLAINE: What did you say?

MATHILDE: Nothing.

VERLAINE: So it's Daddy's idea, is it, Canada, not your idea at
   all? I thought it was a bit subtle for you. What's his plan
   this time? To get me out of the way? To stop me from
   drinking? Or to get my son away from me so I don't
   pervert him with my evil ways? Is that it?

MATHILDE: Paul, don't.
   (*Silence.*)

VERLAINE: I'm sorry, love, sorry. Go on, you'd better go and
   have breakfast. You can tell her it's all right about Canada.

MATHILDE: Can I really?

VERLAINE: Yes.

MATHILDE: Really?

VERLAINE: Yes.

MATHILDE: That's wonderful.

VERLAINE: Here. Give us a kiss.
   (*She does so.*)
   Now, off you go.

MATHILDE: 'Bye.

VERLAINE: Good-bye.

> (*Exit* MATHILDE. VERLAINE *gets dressed, sunk in reflection. Suddenly* RIMBAUD *walks in. He takes in the situation at a glance.*)

RIMBAUD: I see.

VERLAINE: What are you doing here?

RIMBAUD: Nice, was it? A scene of conjugal bliss? I thought she looked a bit flushed.

VERLAINE: How did you get here?

RIMBAUD: I waited until she came down, and went up.

VERLAINE: How did you know which room?

RIMBAUD: I was with you when you booked it.

VERLAINE: Oh, yes.

> (*Silence.*)

RIMBAUD: Well, aren't you going to tell me all about it? You don't usually spare me the hideous details. What about those thighs, paradoxically both moist and silken? What recondite position did you adopt this time?

VERLAINE: I think you'd better go.

RIMBAUD: Oh, I will. I'm more interested in what the position is than in what it was. Just explain it to me, and then I'll go.

VERLAINE: Well, look, not here, she might come back. Let's. . . .

RIMBAUD: No. I want to hear it from you now, and I want you honest and I want you sober. The alternatives are simple. Either you stay in Brussels with me, in which case you send Mathilde back to Paris. Or you go back to Paris with Mathilde, in which case you will kindly leave me some money so that I can get back to France if I want to. That's all. Choose.

> (*Silence.*)

Choose.

VERLAINE: I'm going back to Paris with Mathilde.

RIMBAUD: Right. (*He moves over to the door.*)

VERLAINE: Wait. Wait a minute. Give me a chance to explain.

RIMBAUD: Why should I? I don't need an explanation. I'm not going to waste my time trying to dissuade you, if that's what you want. It's your decision, you made it.

VERLAINE: Listen, don't go. I just want to explain it to you. Sit down a minute.

(RIMBAUD *remains standing, but moves a little nearer to the centre of the stage.*)

RIMBAUD: She might come back.

VERLAINE: Never mind that. It doesn't matter.

(RIMBAUD *smiles and slumps into a chair.*)

Well, she . . . she suggested that we emigrate. To Canada.

RIMBAUD: Did she?

VERLAINE: Yes.

RIMBAUD: Ah.

VERLAINE: Don't you think it's a good idea.

RIMBAUD: No.

VERLAINE: Why not? Look, it's a chance for me. We've got friends out there, it'd be a quiet life, I could write and relax and stop drinking. . . .

RIMBAUD: Leave behind all the bad influences of Europe. . . .

VERLAINE (*after a pause*): Yes. Enjoy the country. . . .

RIMBAUD: Clean living. Back to Rousseau. The noble savage. Paul and Mathilde and their dog Fidèle. Man against the elements. Her idea, was it?

VERLAINE: Yes.

RIMBAUD: Or Daddy's? Nefarious Daddy's? Just before cast-off, Mathilde slips off the boat, leaving Paul impotent and gibbering across the Atlantic ocean, and sexless in Caledonia.

VERLAINE: You don't care about my happiness, do you?

RIMBAUD: No, and neither should you.

(*Silence.*)

VERLAINE: I know I said I'd send her back. But you've never been able to understand how much I love her. This morning, when we made love, it brought back those few months after we were married. She's so beautiful. I came in, this morning, I walked in without knocking and she was lying there, naked, on the bed. She looked so beautiful, when I came in she looked so young and confused. . . .

(*He breaks off.* RIMBAUD *is laughing helplessly.*)

50

VERLAINE: What's the matter?

RIMBAUD: Was she really lying naked on the bed when you arrived?

VERLAINE: Yes.

RIMBAUD: I like that, that's marvellous.

VERLAINE: What do you mean?

RIMBAUD: My estimation for her goes up a long way.

VERLAINE: Why?

RIMBAUD: For realizing what was required, and providing it.

VERLAINE: You are a cynical bastard. She was resting after the journey. She didn't know what time I was arriving.

RIMBAUD: Is she in the habit of lying about the place with no clothes on?

VERLAINE: No. (*Pause.*) Look, what does it matter, anyway?

RIMBAUD: It doesn't. (*Pause.*) She's your wife, you love her, go back to her. (*He gets up.*)

VERLAINE: Christ, I don't know what to do.

(*Silence.* RIMBAUD *begins moving towards the door.*) What do you think?

RIMBAUD: I think it's time I went. I think it's up to you.

VERLAINE: God.

RIMBAUD: I shall await your decision in the hotel.

VERLAINE: Don't go.

RIMBAUD (*smiles*): Perhaps a few drinks would make the whole situation seem a bit clearer.

(*Exit* RIMBAUD. *The light fades on* VERLAINE, *who sits, staring morosely in front of him.*)

CURTAIN

ACT TWO

Scene 1

34–5, Howland Street, London; 24th November, 1872.

VERLAINE *is sitting at the table, writing a letter.* RIMBAUD *is lying on the bed, reading, jotting down the odd note in an exercise book. At first, the conversation is disjointed and sporadic.*

RIMBAUD: What's your greatest fear?

VERLAINE: Mm?

RIMBAUD: I said what's your greatest fear?

VERLAINE: I don't know. I wouldn't like to mislay my balls. (*He continues writing.*) Why, what's yours?

RIMBAUD: That other people will see me as I see them.
(*Silence.*)

RIMBAUD: What time is it they open?

VERLAINE: Not till one o'clock. Ludicrous bloody country.

RIMBAUD: I hate Sundays.

VERLAINE: Especially foggy English Sundays.

RIMBAUD: I've always hated Sundays. Even in Charleville I hated them. We used to march off to High Mass, like a . . . crocodile of penguins. First, Vitalie and Isabelle. Then, Frédéric and I. And bringing up the rear, Mother Rimbe, the mouth of darkness. People used to point us out. She made us hold hands.

I've always felt, contrary to all evidence, that about five o'clock on Sunday evening must have been the time Christ died.
(*Silence.*)

VERLAINE: Chuck us a pear.
(RIMBAUD *does so.*)
Shall I give Lepelletier your love?

RIMBAUD: No.
(*Silence.*)

I love this language. "To put a spurt on", "to tell one's beads", "to skin a flint".

VERLAINE: "William George, of Castle Street, offers a large and varied selection of French letters." Are we going to listen to George Odger this afternoon?

RIMBAUD: Who?

VERLAINE: George Odger, republican. (*He reads from a leaflet.*) ". . . will speak on behalf of the discharged and imprisoned constables." At Hyde Park. "Caution: do not heed the rumours circulated to the contrary and the false reports of the news papers."

RIMBAUD: Doesn't sound very interesting to me.

VERLAINE: At least it's free.

(*Silence.* RIMBAUD *lights his pipe.*)

We're very short at the moment, you know.

RIMBAUD: So you keep saying.

VERLAINE: Don't you think it's time we took a job.

RIMBAUD: I've told you before, I'm not going to take a job. I've got better things to do with my time.

VERLAINE: I mean just a part-time teaching job or something?

RIMBAUD: No. There's nothing to stop you getting a job if you want to.

VERLAINE: I don't want to, I have to.

RIMBAUD: Well, I don't have to. Anyway . . . I'm not staying here much longer.

VERLAINE: You what?

RIMBAUD: Mother was quite right in her letter. It's best if I leave you for a bit.

VERLAINE: Why?

RIMBAUD: Look, do you want a divorce or not?

VERLAINE: Of course not.

RIMBAUD: Well, you're going to get one. They can give her one on desertion, you know, let alone desertion and sodomy.

VERLAINE: I know that.

RIMBAUD: I don't want to get mixed up in it.

VERLAINE: That's why it's better if you stay here. I mean, if you leave now, it'll be an admission of guilt, won't it? Obviously. The only answer is to bluff it out. That's why I've told

53

Lepelletier in this letter to tell Mauté we're ready to submit
to a medical examination, if he likes.

RIMBAUD: Are you mad?

VERLAINE: No, look, I've phrased it carefully. . . .

RIMBAUD: Suppose he says yes?

(*Silence.*)

VERLAINE: He won't.

RIMBAUD: I'm leaving next week.

VERLAINE: He couldn't possibly.

RIMBAUD: You don't think he made this accusation because he
was looking for a way to liven up the long winter evenings,
do you? He made it because he knows.

VERLAINE: Nonsense, it was a theatrical gesture.

RIMBAUD: You always judge people from a literary standpoint,
which means that your assessment of their motives is
usually inaccurate.

VERLAINE: Anyway, it's him that's in the wrong. How many
times have I asked for my things back from that house, and
he's still got them there.

RIMBAUD: You're in the wrong.

VERLAINE (*suddenly coldly angry*): All right, I'm in the wrong, if
you say so, then that's established, isn't it? Now perhaps
you'll let me get on and finish my letter.

(RIMBAUD *doesn't answer.* VERLAINE *continues writing.*)

RIMBAUD. Shall we forgive God?

VERLAINE: What?

RIMBAUD: Shall we forgive him for what he's done to us? Or for
what we've done to ourselves? As it's Sunday.

VERLAINE: Is he responsible?

RIMBAUD: Or irresponsible? As a writer, is it my job to create a
pleasanter world than God has created?

VERLAINE: No, it's your job to create a world which has some
bearing on truth.

RIMBAUD: I can do that, and my world will still be pleasanter
than God's. In fact, I can't fail, because in my world the
pain doesn't hurt.

VERLAINE: But your world is only a metaphor.

RIMBAUD: Perhaps God should have been content with a

metaphor.

VERLAINE: He uses metaphor when he feels inclined. What
about the Crucifixion? What about the Resurrection?

RIMBAUD: Sheer nepotism.

VERLAINE (*smiling*): Why be facetious?

RIMBAUD: I feel like it. Why take on the role of God's advocate?

VERLAINE: I feel like it.

RIMBAUD: Strange, isn't it?

(*Silence.*)

And so, ladies and gentlemen, in spite of the spirited
defence of M. Paul Verlaine, and the specious and indeed
frivolous arguments used by M. Arthur Rimbaud for the
prosecution, the court has no option but to find the defendant,
God, alias Jehovah, alias the Lord of Hosts, guilty of crimes
against humanity, and to sentence him to be forgiven.

My eyes sting.

The court has arrived at this whimsical decision, ladies and
gentlemen, for a variety of reasons, if one may presume to
rationalize the intentionally irrational. To begin with, it
was goaded by the defendant's repeated assertions that he
moved in a mysterious way, into showing that it too was a
body not incapable of enigma. Secondly, the defendant was
tactless enough to imply that as he had created the court
and all its members, he could perfectly well uncreate them
or even plunge them into everlasting hellfire at any
moment. This, it was felt, constituted extreme contempt of
court, and was largely responsible for the imposition of the
maximum penalty. And thirdly, it's Sunday, and the court
is bored.

I shall leave next week.

VERLAINE: We'll discuss it later, shall we?

RIMBAUD: I doubt it.

(VERLAINE *finishes his letter.*)

VERLAINE: Course it won't go today, even if I post it. The post
is terrible in this country.

RIMBAUD: Are they open yet?

VERLAINE: Are we going to listen to Mr. Odger?

RIMBAUD: Drinks first.

VERLAINE: Just a minute, I must line my stomach first. (*He pours himself a glass of milk and drinks.*) Ugh. It's horrible. I was wrong about Mauté. He is of some use to the nation. They milk him for export. (*He laughs and goes over to look out of the window.*) It's very foggy. (*He puts on his overcoat.*) One evening, I set out to assassinate Napoléon III. I was rather drunk, and I'd decided things had gone far enough. Unfortunately I never managed it.

(*They smile at each other with some tenderness.*)

CURTAIN

Scene 2

8, Great College Street, London; 3rd July, 1873.

Another anonymous London bed-sitter. VERLAINE *is opening a bottle of wine,* RIMBAUD *is lying on his bed, doing nothing.*

VERLAINE: Do you realize we've known each other almost two years now?

RIMBAUD: Is it autumn already?

VERLAINE: No, no, summer.

RIMBAUD: Seems more like ten.

VERLAINE: Not that you can tell the difference in England.

RIMBAUD: And how long is it since we got back to London?

VERLAINE: Not more than five weeks.

RIMBAUD: God, life will never end.

(VERLAINE *pours wine into two glasses, takes one over to* RIMBAUD.)

VERLAINE: A lot can happen in two years.

RIMBAUD: A lot can happen in ten minutes. But it rarely does.

VERLAINE: Mind you, it's less than three years ago I got married.

RIMBAUD: I thought you weren't going to mention that again.

VERLAINE: I was only. . . .

RIMBAUD: Well, don't.

56

VERLAINE: I'm sorry.

RIMBAUD: More.

(VERLAINE *goes over and pours him out some more wine.*)

VERLAINE: There have been good times, though, haven't there? I mean, we have been happy.

RIMBAUD: When?

VERLAINE: You know. Even you must grudgingly admit we've been happy sometimes.

RIMBAUD: I've told you before, I'm too intelligent to be happy.

VERLAINE: I remember you telling me once, when we were trying to get some sleep in a ditch in Belgium, that you'd never been so happy in your life.

RIMBAUD: Kindly spare us another bout of your lying and utterly revolting nostalgia.

VERLAINE: Why do you take such pleasure in being unhappy?

RIMBAUD: I assure you I get no more pleasure from pain than I do from pleasure.

VERLAINE: You've become perversely addicted to pessimism.

RIMBAUD: More.

VERLAINE: Get it yourself.

RIMBAUD: You're getting a bit assertive in your old age.

(*He gets up to pour himself some more wine.* VERLAINE *wanders over to the window.*)

VERLAINE: It's still raining.

(*Silence.*)

You're right about old age. I shall be thirty next birthday. Thirty. What a horrible thought.

RIMBAUD: Disgusting.

VERLAINE: And you're getting on. Nearly nineteen.

RIMBAUD: I begin to despair.

VERLAINE: Why?

RIMBAUD: When I was young and golden and infallible, I saw the future with some clarity. I saw the failings of my predecessors and saw, I thought, how they could be avoided. I knew it would be difficult, but I thought that all I needed was experience, and I could turn myself into the philosopher's stone, and create new colours and new flowers, new languages and a new God, and everything to gold. Thou shalt, I said to myself, adopting the appropriate apocalyptic style, be reviled and persecuted as any prophet, but at the last thou shalt prevail.

But before long I realized it was impossible to be a doubting prophet. If you are a prophet you may be optimistic or pessimistic as the fancy takes you, but you may never be anything less than certain. And I found I had tortured myself and punished my brain and poked among my entrails to discover something that people do not believe, or do not wish to believe, or would be foolish to believe. And with the lyricism of self-pity, I turned to the mirror and said Lord, what shall I do, for there is no love in the world and no hope, and I can do nothing about it, God, I can do no more than you have done, and I am in Hell, tormented by laughter and locked in the sterility of paradox.

Not that I haven't said all this before.

I have, and clearly a new code is called for. And in these last few weeks when you may have been thinking, I've just been lying here in a state of paralysed sloth, you've actually been quite right. But bubbling beneath the surface and rising slowly through the layers of indifference has been a new system. Harden up. Reject romanticism. Abandon rhetoric. Get it right.

And now I've got it right and seen where my attempt to conquer the world has led me.

VERLAINE: Where?

RIMBAUD: Here. My search for universal experience has led me here. To lead an idle, pointless life of poverty, as the minion of a bald, ugly, ageing, drunken lyric poet, who clings on to me because his wife won't take him back.

(*Silence. At first* VERLAINE *is too astonished to speak.*)

VERLAINE: How can you bring yourself to say a thing like that?

RIMBAUD: It's easy. It's the truth. You're here, living like this, because you have to be. It's your life. Drink and sex and a kind of complacent melancholy and enough money to soak yourself oblivious every night. That's your limit. But I'm here because I choose to be.

VERLAINE: Oh yes?

RIMBAUD: Yes.

VERLAINE: And why exactly?

RIMBAUD: What do you mean, why?

VERLAINE: Why exactly did you choose to come back to London with me? What was the intellectual basis of your choice?

RIMBAUD: This is a question I repeatedly ask myself.

VERLAINE: No doubt you regarded it as another stage in your private Odyssey. Only by plunging ever deeper, if I may mix my myths, will you attain the right to graze on the upper slopes of Parnassus.

RIMBAUD: Your attack is unusually coherent this morning.

VERLAINE: My theory differs from yours. My theory is that you are like Musset.

RIMBAUD: What?

VERLAINE: Rather a provocative comparison, don't you think, in view of your continual attacks on the wretched man?

RIMAUD: Explain it.

VERLAINE: Well, I simply mean that like Musset or one of Musset's heroes, you tried on the cloak of vice, and now it's stuck to your skin. You came back here with me because you wanted to, and because you needed to.

RIMBAUD: Well now, that's quite original for you, even though you have made your customary mistake.

VERLAINE: What's that?

RIMBAUD: Getting carried away by an idea because it's aesthetically plausible rather than actually true.

VERLAINE: Oh, there are less subtle reasons for your putting up with me.

RIMBAUD: Such as?

VERLAINE: Such as the fact that I support you.
(*Silence.*)

RIMBAUD: Your mind is almost as ugly as your body.
(*Silence. They look at each other.* VERLAINE *struggles with himself for a moment, then, suddenly, his face goes blank and he strides across the stage.*)

RIMBAUD (*uneasily*): Where are you going?

VERLAINE: To the kitchen. It's lunchtime.

(*Exit* VERLAINE. RIMBAUD *pours himself a drink rather shakily, and swallows it. He seems puzzled. A moment later,* VERLAINE *enters again, carrying in one hand, a herring, and in the other, a bottle of oil.* RIMBAUD *looks at him, then bursts out laughing.* VERLAINE *scarcely responds.*)

RIMBAUD: God, you look such a cunt.

(VERLAINE *doesn't answer. Instead, he puts the herring and the bottle of oil down on the table, and strides across the stage, away from the kitchen.*)
Where are you going?
(*Exit* VERLAINE.)
Where are you going? (*He looks frightened and vulnerable.*)

CURTAIN

Scene 3

A hotel room in Brussels; 10th July, 1873.
RIMBAUD *is packing. He looks tired and rather sad. The door bursts open and* VERLAINE *enters. He is drunk, which in his case means over-excitement and a certain belligerence, rather than incoherence or physical unsteadiness.*

RIMBAUD: Where have you been?

VERLAINE: Out. I went, I went to the Spanish Embassy again, to see if they would change their minds. But they wouldn't, it's ridiculous, it's bloody ridiculous. I'm willing to fight, I said, and die for your cause, you can't afford to turn away volunteers. But they said they weren't taking on any foreigners. Then, I said, you deserve to lose the bloody war, and I hope you do.

RIMBAUD: And were you at the Spanish Embassy all morning?

VERLAINE: No.

RIMBAUD: You're drunk.

VERLAINE: I have yes had a few drinks.

(*Silence.* VERLAINE *notices that* RIMBAUD *is packing.*)

What are you doing?

RIMBAUD: I'm packing.

VERLAINE: Where are you going?

RIMBAUD: I've told you already, I'm going back to Paris. And if you'll kindly give me some money for the fare, I shall leave this evening.

VERLAINE: No, listen, listen, we're going back to London.

RIMBAUD: We are not going back to London.

VERLAINE: Yes, look, I've been thinking it over this morning, it's by far the best idea.

RIMBAUD: Then why did you go to the Spanish Embassy?

VERLAINE: I didn't.

(*Silence.*)

RIMBAUD: I am going back to Paris.

VERLAINE: It won't happen again, look, I'll never walk out on you again like that, I promise.

RIMBAUD: No, you won't.

VERLAINE: Don't go. Just wait another day or two and think it over.

RIMBAUD: I've thought it over.

VERLAINE: Or else, what about this, I had another idea this morning. I thought I might go to Paris.

RIMBAUD: What?

VERLAINE: I thought I might go to Paris and try to find Mathilde.

RIMBAUD (*after considering this*): Well, all right, I don't mind travelling with you.

VERLAINE: No, no, you would stay here in Brussels.

RIMBAUD: Are you mad?

VERLAINE: No, don't you see, it would be absolutely fatal if you came back with me. She'd never take me back.

RIMBAUD: I doubt she will anyway.

VERLAINE: Well then, I'll come back to Brussels, and we can go back to London.

RIMBAUD: You're out of your mind.

VERLAINE: Do you realize what day it is tomorrow?

RIMBAUD: Friday.

VERLAINE: It's my anniversary, it's our third anniversary. And I

61

haven't seen her, my wife, for almost a year. A year ago, here in Brussels, we made love, and I haven't seen her since. And I haven't seen my son for more than a year. She won't answer my letters. Do you know that I wrote to her last week, and told her if she didn't come to Brussels within three days, I'd commit suicide? And she didn't even answer.

RIMBAUD: Ah, but then you didn't commit suicide.

VERLAINE: I suppose you think that's funny.

RIMBAUD: No, it's pitiful. How many people did you write and tell you were going to commit suicide? I'm surprised you didn't send out invitations.

VERLAINE: How can you be so callous?

RIMBAUD: Callous? You abandon me in London with no money at all and then summon me to Brussels and expect me to hang about while you decide whether you're going to go back to your wife, join the army, or shoot yourself. Then, when you fail to achieve any of these aims, as you undoubtedly will, you expect me to go back to London again.

I'm not going to. It's all over. I'm leaving you.

VERLAINE: You can't. You can't. (*Paces up and down for a moment.*) Where's mother?

RIMBAUD: Next door, I suppose, in her room. I asked her to let me have some money, but she wouldn't give it to me until you came back. I'll go and ask her again.

VERLAINE: No, no, wait a minute. Look, I'll give you the money. I just want to talk to you a minute. (*He paces up and down, smiles nervously at* RIMBAUD.) Hot, isn't it?

I think we can start again. I don't think it would be too difficult to go back to the beginning. I know it's my fault, all the trouble we've had recently, but it's only because of Mathilde, because I still loved Mathilde. It's finished with her now, I know I shall never see her again. Look, it's summer. Don't you remember last summer, when we set out, how wonderful it was. I remember evenings. . . . There's no need to go back to London if you don't want to. We could go south. Late summer on the Mediterranean,

we could live more cheaply there, we wouldn't need to
work, we could dedicate ourselves to warmth. Or Africa,
we could go to North Africa, I know you've always
wanted to go to Africa. Just for a month and then make up
your mind.

Look at the sun.

(*Long silence.*)

RIMBAUD: No.

VERLAINE: Why not?

RIMBAUD (*gently*): I can't. It's no good. It's too late.

VERLAINE: No, it's not. I promise you it's not. You know if you
leave me, you'll kill me. I can't bear to be alone. I don't
exist without someone else. I don't care if you stay with
me out of pity, as long as you stay.

RIMBAUD: I can't.

VERLAINE: Why not? What more can I say to make you stay?
Don't you care? Have you no idea of what this means to
me?

RIMBAUD: Oh, for God's sake, stop whining.

(*Silence.* VERLAINE *goes over to look out of the window. He
mops his brow with a handkerchief.*)

VERLAINE: It's very hot.

RIMBAUD: I should take your coat off.

VERLAINE: I will. (*He slips his coat off, walks over to the door,
and hangs it up.*) I did some shopping this morning. (*He
takes something out of his pocket, and turns towards*
RIMBAUD.) I bought a gun. (*He points a revolver at*
RIMBAUD.)

RIMBAUD: What for?

VERLAINE: For you. And for me. For everybody.

RIMBAUD: I hope you bought plenty of ammunition.

(VERLAINE *moves a chair in front of the door, and sits astride
it, pointing the revolver at* RIMBAUD *over the back of the
chair.* RIMBAUD *leans against the opposite wall, smiling.*)

VERLAINE: I'm not going to let you go, you know.

RIMBAUD: Well, this is rather an entertaining number. We
haven't seen this one before.

VERLAINE (*cries out*): I'll kill you!

RIMBAUD: Oh, get a grip of your knickers.

(*Silence.*)

VERLAINE: Have you forgotten what you said in your letter?

RIMBAUD: What letter?

VERLAINE: The letter you wrote me last week, the day after I left you.

RIMBAUD: It's of no relevance.

VERLAINE: Oh, yes it is. You apologized. You begged me to come back. You said it was all your fault. You said you loved me. You said it would be all right in the future. You said you were crying as you wrote. I could see your tears on the paper.

RIMBAUD: Well, I didn't have any money, did I? That was before I thought of pawning your clothes.

(VERLAINE *springs to his feet, shaking with rage. He raises the revolver and fires at* RIMBAUD, *then, apparently stunned by the noise of the retort, fires again into the floor.* RIMBAUD *is clutching at his left wrist, and staring at it in amazement and horror, as blood pours down over his hand. He shies away, as* VERLAINE *moves towards him.*)

VERLAINE: Oh, God, I'm sorry, I didn't mean to.

RIMBAUD: Look what you've done.

VERLAINE: I'm sorry, I didn't mean to.

RIMBAUD: Look.

(VERLAINE *bursts into tears. He tries to give* RIMBAUD *the revolver.*)

VELAINE: Oh, for God's sake, kill me, kill me, shoot me.

RIMBAUD: What?

VERLAINE: Shoot me.

RIMBAUD: How can I, you silly bugger, you've just blown a hole in my hand.

(*A furious banging at the door and a female voice shouting:* 'Paul, Paul'. . . . VERLAINE *drops the revolver.* RIMBAUD *begins to laugh hysterically.*)

VERLAINE: Oh God, what have I done?

RIMBAUD: You missed.

(*Blackout.*)

CURTAIN

Scene 4

Brussels, 10th–19th July, 1873.
This scene is constructed from fragments of VERLAINE's *trial.*
On one side of the stage, RIMBAUD *lies in bed, his arm in a sling.*
VERLAINE *sits on the other side of the stage, in court. The magistrate,*
JUDGE THÉODORE T'SERSTEVENS, *and his* CLERK *commute from one*
side of the stage to the other. When the scene opens, the CLERK *is*
taking down RIMBAUD's *statement.*

RIMBAUD : . . . When the wound had been dressed, the three of
us returned to the hotel. Verlaine asked me continually not
to leave him and to stay with him; but I refused to agree
and left the hotel about seven o'clock in the evening,
accompanied by Verlaine and his mother. Not far from the
Place Rouppe, Verlaine went on a few paces ahead and
then turned towards me: I saw him put his hand in his
pocket to get his revolver, so I turned and walked away. I
met a police officer and told him what had happened to
me, and he invited Verlaine to accompany him to the
police station.

If Verlaine had let me leave freely, I would have taken
no action against him for the wound he inflicted on
me. . . .

(*The* CLERK *crosses the stage to join the* JUDGE *and*
VERLAINE.)
CLERK (*reads*): Statement of Mme Verlaine, the defendant's
mother: For about two years, M. Rimbaud has lived at the
expense of my son, who has often had occasion to
complain of his spiteful and disagreeable character. . . .
When his wound had been dressed at the Saint-Jean
Hospital, Rimbaud expressed the desire to return to Paris,
and I gave him 20 francs, because he had no money. Then,
on the way to the station, he asked the police officer to

arrest my son, who bore him no malice and had acted in a
moment of distraction. . . .

(*Pause.* VERLAINE *rises.*)

VERLAINE: . . . I swear to tell the whole truth and nothing but
the truth, so help me God and all His saints.

JUDGE: Have you any previous convictions?

VERLAINE: No.

JUDGE: What is the motive behind your presence in Brussels?

VERLAINE: I was hoping that my wife might come and join me
here, as she had already done so on one occasion since our
separation.

JUDGE: I fail to see how the departure of a friend could have
cast you into such despair. Did there not exist between you
and Rimbaud other relations besides those of friendship?

VERLAINE: No; this is a suggestion slanderously invented by my
wife and her family to harm me; I have been accused of
this in my wife's petition for divorce.

JUDGE: Both doctors have testified that on the basis of their
examination they are satisfied that you have recently
indulged in both active and passive sodomy.

VERLAINE: Yes.

JUDGE: Then do you deny that you are a practising sodomist?

VERLAINE: The word is sodomite. . . .

(*Pause. The* JUDGE *and the* CLERK *cross the stage to
interrogate* RIMBAUD.)

RIMBAUD: I swear to tell the whole truth and nothing but
the truth, so help me God and all His saints.

JUDGE: What did you live on in London?

RIMBAUD: Principally on the money Mme Verlaine sent to her
son. We also taught French together, but that didn't bring
in much, perhaps a dozen francs a week towards the end.

JUDGE: Are you aware of the reasons behind Verlaine's dis-
agreements with his wife?

RIMBAUD: Verlaine didn't want his wife to go on living in her
father's house.

JUDGE: But did she not also object to your . . . friendship with

66

Verlaine?

RIMBAUD: Yes, she even accuses us of immoral relations; but I scarcely think it's worth bothering to deny such allegations.

(*Pause. The* JUDGE *and the* CLERK *return to the court, where the* CLERK *reads* RIMBAUD's *final statement, as the lights dim.*)

CLERK: . . . I, the undersigned, Arthur Rimbaud, aged 19, man of letters, generally domiciled at Charleville (the Ardennes, France), declare it to be the truth that on Thursday, the 10th inst., at the moment when M. Paul Verlaine fired at me and wounded me slightly in the left wrist, M. Verlaine was in such a complete state of drunkenness, that he had no idea of what he was doing.

That I am utterly convinced that when he bought the revolver, M. Verlaine had no hostile intention towards me, and that there was no criminal premeditation in his action;

That the cause of M. Verlaine's drunkenness related simply to his difficulties with Mme Verlaine, his wife;

I further declare that I am willing to withdraw from any criminal, correctional or civil action against him, and as from today renounce the benefits of any proceedings which may be brought against M. Verlaine by the Public Prosecutor arising from this matter. . . .

JUDGE: . . . The accused, Paul-Marie Verlaine, is committed for trial at the criminal court, charged under article 399 of the Penal Code, of grievous bodily harm. The preliminary examination is closed. . . .

CLERK (*in the darkness*): Paul-Marie Verlaine, the court finds you guilty of grievous bodily harm and sentences you to a fine of 200 francs and 2 years' imprisonment.

CURTAIN

Scene 5

The Black Forest, near Stuttgart; 28th February, 1875.

The curtain goes up on an empty stage. The scene suggests a clearing in a wood by a river. Sounds of laughter offstage. Presently RIMBAUD *enters, a little better dressed than in previous scenes. It is evening. Moonlight.*

RIMBAUD: This way.

(He laughs. VERLAINE *enters.)*

When was this, anyway?

VERLAINE: Earlier this month.

(RIMBAUD *laughs again.*)

RIMBAUD: And they threw you out?

VERLAINE: Certainly not. After a week the Father Superior and I agreed that it wasn't really the life for me.

RIMBAUD: This'll do. *(He squats down on the ground and lights his clay pipe.)* And what led you to believe that you were cut out to be a Trappist monk?

VERLAINE: I don't know. Perhaps it was nostalgia for prison. It was terrible coming out, you know. I'd got used to the quiet and the routine, they treated me very well, and I was sober and able to do a lot of good work. Then, when I came out and couldn't even get to see Mathilde's lawyer, let alone Mathilde, I thought the best thing to do might be to . . . withdraw. To a monastery, to live a quiet, simple life with God.

RIMBAUD: But it turned out to be a teetotal order.

VERLAINE: I told you I got used to being sober in prison.

RIMBAUD: I'm pleased to see the situation is not wholly irreversible.

VERLAINE: Well, tonight is different. Tonight is a celebration. It's really . . . wonderful to see you again. *(Pause.)* After all this time. *(Pause.)* I hope you never thought . . . that I was angry with you.

RIMBAUD: No.

68

VERLAINE: I mean, I know you had no idea that I might get put away for so long, I certainly . . . forgave you for it.

RIMBAUD: Did you?

VERLAINE: Oh, yes.

RIMBAUD: I didn't forgive you.

VERLAINE: What for?

RIMBAUD: For missing.

(VERLAINE *laughs uneasily. Silence.*)

VERLAINE: It's very pleasant here.

RIMBAUD: Im Schwarzwald.

VERLAINE: How is your German?

RIMBAUD: Flourishing.

(*Silence.*)

VERLAINE: Not very warm, is it?

RIMBAUD: Why did you come here?

VERLAINE: What?

RIMBAUD: I want to know your reason for coming here.

VERLAINE: Well . . . to see you, of course. I wanted to talk to you, to discuss certain things with you.

RIMBAUD: You want us to love each other in Jesus, am I right?

VERLAINE: Well. . . .

RIMBAUD: All right, I'm listening, tell me about it.

VERLAINE: It's very difficult to talk seriously if you're going to be so aggressive. I've changed, you know.

RIMBAUD: Go on, talk seriously, never mind what I say. A missionary should be prepared to meet aggression from the unenlightened. Tell me about your conversion. Was it a bit of an occasion? Was there a celestial voice, which spake unto you, saying: "Paul, Paul of Brussels, you are my servant in whom I am ill pleased, what do you propose to do about it?" I've always wanted to get my teeth into a celestial voice.

VERLAINE: Recently it occurred to me that your anger and disgust prove how ready you are for conversion. And anyway I often think you do believe in God. Even in the old days, when you used to paint up "Sod God" in the urinals in Paris, you must have had some faith. You can't blaspheme if you don't believe.

RIMBAUD: No, you're wrong. You couldn't blaspheme if nobody believed. Your own feelings have nothing to do with it.

VERLAINE: I just want you to follow my example. The day of my conversion was one of the happiest of my life. It was the day the governor came and told me Mathilde had been granted a legal separation. I lay down and looked at my life, and there was nothing, nothing. It seemed to me the only thing I could do was submit myself to God, and ask Him to forgive me, and help me to face my situation. And He did. I promise you He did.

RIMBAUD (*kindly*): Don't let's talk about it any more.

VERLAINE: Why not?

RIMBAUD: It's dangerous.

VERLAINE: But I want you to find some direction to your life. I want God to help you to achieve your aims.

RIMBAUD: Aims? I have no aims.

VERLAINE: Well, I mean your writing.

RIMBAUD: I've stopped writing.

VERLAINE: What?

RIMBAUD: I have stopped writing.

VERLAINE: I don't understand. . . .

RIMBAUD: Well, let me put it another way: I no longer write.

VERLAINE: Yes, but why not?

RIMBAUD: Because I have nothing more to say. If I ever had anything to say in the first place.

VERLAINE: How can you say that?

(RIMBAUD *laughs at* VERLAINE'*s unhappy choice of words.*)
How can you?

RIMBAUD: Well, as you know, I started life as a self-appointed visionary, and creator of a new literature. But as time wore on, and it took me longer and longer to write less and less, and I looked back at some of the absurdities of my earlier work, at some of the things I thought were so good when I wrote them, I saw it was pointless to go on. The world is too old, there's nothing new, it's all been said. Anything that can be put into words is not worth putting into words.

VERLAINE: The truth is always worth putting into words.

RIMBAUD: The truth is too limited to be interesting.

VERLAINE: What do you mean?—Truth is infinite.

RIMBAUD: If you're referring to the truth that was revealed to you in prison by an angel of the Lord, you may be wrong. After all, what makes you think it's any truer than the rather different views you asserted with equal confidence three years ago?

VERLAINE: Well, obviously one develops.

RIMBAUD: And have you developed?

VERLAINE: Yes.

(*Long silence.*)

RIMBAUD: Then, here in the wilderness, I offer you an archetypal choice—the choice between my body and my soul.

VERLAINE: What?

(*Long silence.*)

RIMBAUD: Choose.

VERLAINE: Your body.

(*Silence.*)

RIMBAUD: See, the ninety-eight wounds of Our Saviour burst and bleed.

VERLAINE: Please.

RIMBAUD: So you didn't come here to convert me.

VERLAINE: No.

RIMBAUD: And the iron glove conceals a velvet hand.

(VERLAINE *moves towards* RIMBAUD, *touches his shoulder.*) Don't.

(*Silence.*)

So God turned out to be a poor substitute for Mathilde and me, suffering, as he does, from certain tangible disadvantages.

VERLAINE: Surely my sins are a matter for my own conscience.

RIMBAUD: They would be if you had one.

VERLAINE: Anyway, why should it worry you?

RIMBAUD: Because I hate your miserable weakness.

VERLAINE: Is overcoming my conscience weakness? Or strength?

RIMBAUD: Don't be absurd.

(*Silence.*)

VERLAINE: But I see no clash between loving God and loving you.

71

RIMBAUD: Come on, let's go back.

VERLAINE: No, listen, I sat in my cell and thought how much love I had in me, and how happy we could be, it should be easy, it should be the easiest thing in the world, why isn't it?

RIMBAUD: It never worked with us. And it will never work for either of us.

VERLAINE: Of course it will. Why should you think that? Why are you so destructive?

RIMBAUD: Probably because I no longer have any sympathy for you.

VERLAINE: Don't you feel anything for me?

RIMBAUD: Only a kind of mild contempt.

VERLAINE: But how can you change like that? How is it possible?

RIMBAUD: I don't know.

VERLAINE: I wanted us to go away together.

RIMBAUD: Yes.

VERLAINE: What are you going to do?

RIMBAUD: I'm going to finish learning German. And then I'm going to leave Europe. Alone.

VERLAINE: What about me?

RIMBAUD: You'll have to go away and find somebody else.

VERLAINE: I can't. Please. (*He puts his arms round* RIMBAUD.) Please.

RIMBAUD: Let me go.

(VERLAINE *clings on to him.* RIMBAUD *speaks, as he has done throughout this last exchange, with great weariness.*)
Let go.

VERLAINE: Please.

RIMBAUD *hits* VERLAINE *hard, stunning him. He hits him again, carefully and methodically, until he collapses in an untidy heap.* RIMBAUD *straightens him out almost tenderly, then stands looking down at him for a moment.*)

RIMBAUD (*quietly*): Good-bye. (*He exits.*)

CURTAIN

Scene 6

A café in Paris; 29th February, 1892.

It is early evening and the rather squalid café, is not very full. Presently VERLAINE *enters. He is now 47, but looks much older, a derelict carnal hulk. His clothes are correct, much as they were in the first scene of the play, but worn and shabby. He has a walking-stick, and limps heavily, dragging his left leg behind him. He is accompanied by* EUGÉNIE KRANTZ, *who is about the same age as he is. She is an ageing prostitute, plump and supremely unattractive. Her accent sounds like a crude parody of* RIMBAUD'S.

VERLAINE: Evening.
>   (*A few muttered replies. He and* EUGÉNIE *sit at one of the tables.*)
>   Absinthe, please. Two.
>   (*The* BARMAN *nods, pours drinks behind the bar.*)
>   God, I'm tired.

EUGÉNIE (*sniggers*): Not surprised.

VERLAINE: You're beautiful, Eugénie.

EUGÉNIE: I know. (*She laughs raucously.*)

VERLAINE: Don't let anyone tell you different. If I think you're beautiful, then you're beautiful.
>   (*The* BARMAN *brings the drinks.*)

BARMAN: Someone been in to see you this afternoon, M. Verlaine.

VERLAINE: Who?

BARMAN: A young lady. She didn't leave her name.

VERLAINE: A young lady?

BARMAN: Well, in her thirties, I suppose. She seemed very keen to see you, so I said you'd be sure to be in later, and she said she'd come back. She said it was quite important.

VERLAINE: Thanks.
>   (*The* BARMAN *turns away.*)
>   Just a minute. . . . What did she look like?

73

BARMAN: Oh, not bad, monsieurs, not bad.

VERLAINE: Thanks.

(*Silence.*)

EUGÉNIE: Who is it?

VERLAINE: What?

EUGÉNIE: Who is it?

VERLAINE: How should I know?

EUGÉNIE: It can't be Esther, it's too young for her. So it must be someone else.

VERLAINE: I told you I haven't seen Esther since I came out of hospital.

EUGÉNIE: You told me! Who is it?

VERLAINE: I don't know.

(*Silence.*)

It must be some business matter.

EUGÉNIE: Business, eh?

VERLAINE: Yes. I'd appreciate it if you'd let me talk to her alone when she comes.

EUGÉNIE: Oh, charming, that is. Lovely. I'm supposed to go and sit on my own, am I, while you talk to your new girl-friends?

VERLAINE: I promise you I don't know who it is, and if it's a business matter, I'd rather talk to her alone.

EUGÉNIE (*a threat*): I shall go and talk to that gentleman over there.

VERLAINE: Well, you must do as you like.

EUGÉNIE: Perhaps he'll turn out a bit more respectful than you are.

(*Silence.*)

VERLAINE: Two more, please.

(*The* BARMAN *comes over, and pours the drinks.*)

Can you let me have some money, please?

EUGÉNIE: Eh?

VERLAINE: I haven't any money on me.

EUGÉNIE: Well, don't ask me for money.

VERLAINE: Look, Eugénie, I'm not feeling very well, and I don't want to argue with you. Now will you kindly give me some money.

EUGÉNIE: You haven't done any work today.

VERLAINE: I haven't been feeling very well.

EUGÉNIE: Well, if you don't do any work, you can't expect to be paid.

VERLAINE: Look, it's my money.

EUGÉNIE: It wouldn't be much longer if I let you get your hands on it.

VERLAINE: I just want a few. . . .

EUGÉNIE: No.

(ISABELLE RIMBAUD *enters. She is 31, very respectably dressed in mourning, and already something of an old maid. There is some resemblance between her and her brother, but this is most noticeable when she speaks—with* RIMBAUD's *soft provincial accent. She goes over and has a word with the* BARMAN, *who points out* VERLAINE *to her. He is still arguing with* EUGÉNIE *in a violent undertone.*)

VERLAINE: Now, listen, Eugénie, if you don't give me some money at once, there'll be trouble, do you understand?

EUGÉNIE: I haven't got any money with me. So you'll have to do without, won't you?

VERLAINE: You're making me very angry.

EUGÉNIE: Anyway, here comes your girl-friend, by the look of it. So I'll be leaving you. (*She gets up, then leans forward and speaks in a venomous whisper.*) And if you don't come back tonight, you'll find your things in the street. (*She leaves him, and while he is speaking to* ISABELLE, *she joins one of the men sitting at a table at the back of the stage.* VERLAINE *rises, turns to meet* ISABELLE.)

ISABELLE (*tentatively*): M. Verlaine?

VERLAINE: At your service, mademoiselle.

ISABELLE: I am Isabelle Rimbaud.

VERLAINE: Pardon? (*He sinks into his chair.*)

ISABELLE: I am Isabelle Rimbaud. I am M. Arthur Rimbaud's sister.

VERLAINE: Of course, er, of course, please sit down, mademoiselle. You must excuse me for being so rude, but I find it difficult to stand, I'm having . . . a lot of trouble with my knee. (ISABELLE *sits.*)

75

I heard, we heard the tragic news a couple of months ago. I could hardly believe it, he was so young. And then, he'd been reported dead before, you know, earlier. I was deeply . . . affected by his death, although I hadn't seen him for so long.

ISABELLE: I didn't know whether you'd heard.

VERLAINE: Is it true . . . is it true he had to have his leg amputated?

ISABELLE: Yes.

(*Silence.*)

I'll get straight to the point, M. Verlaine, I don't have very much time.

VERLAINE: You look a bit like him, you know. Your eyes . . . are not unlike his.

ISABELLE: So I've been told.

VERLAINE: Would you like a drink?

ISABELLE: No thank you very much. It's really a business matter I want to discuss with you. M. Vanier said you might be able to help me.

VERLAINE: Well, I'll do what I can.

ISABELLE: On the day my brother died, a volume of his poems was published in Paris, wasn't it?

VERLAINE: You mean *The Reliquary*?

ISABELLE: That's right. The publication was completely un-authorized, and there was an anonymous preface full of the most outrageous and libellous statements, which claimed to be a biography of my brother. My mother and I were very upset by it.

VERLAINE: Yes, well, er, I believe M. Genonceaux is the man you should see about this. He's the editor.

ISABELLE: I know. I haven't been able to get hold of M. Genonceaux.

VERLAINE: Anyway, the book's now been withdrawn from circulation.

ISABELLE: I know. But my mother and I are anxious to prevent anything like this from happening again. And M. Vanier said you might be able to help us.

VERLAINE: I? How?

ISABELLE: Well, I understand you have a large number of my
brother's manuscripts.

VERLAINE: I have . . . some, yes.

ISABELLE: My mother and I would be very grateful if you'd
return them.

(*Silence.*)

VERLAINE: I've always . . . used the utmost discretion in everything concerning your brother. I think I can say that I've
always defended his interests. Since his name began to be
well known, various newspapers and magazines have
printed forgeries, you know, and I've made myself
responsible for putting a stop to it and making sure that
everything that comes out under his name is his work.

ISABELLE: I didn't know his name was all that well known.

VERLAINE: Oh, yes.

ISABELLE: That makes it even more vital that we collect up all
his manuscripts. Perhaps I should explain our intentions to
you. Did you know he was converted before he died?

VERLAINE: Converted?

ISABELLE: Yes. I reasoned with him and prayed for him for
weeks while he was ill and about a fortnight before he died,
he asked to be confessed. After that, we prayed together
every day, and the chaplain said that he had never
encountered faith as strong as Arthur's. Do you know, in
spite of the tragic circumstances, the day Arthur asked for
the chaplain was one of the happiest of my life.

VERLAINE: So he took the last Sacraments?

ISABELLE: No, unfortunately they weren't able to give him
communion, because he couldn't keep anything down, and
they were afraid there might be an involuntary sacrilege.
But I know his soul was saved.

VERLAINE (*without irony*): That must be a great comfort.

ISABELLE: Yes. Anyway, you'll appreciate now how important
it is for my mother and I to get hold of his writings.

VERLAINE: Er. . . ?

ISABELLE: The point is, M. Verlaine, to speak frankly, a number
of the poems he wrote in extreme youth were rather . . .
indecent, and in some cases even profane. He would never

77

have wished to be remembered for them. My mother and I plan to as it were separate the wheat from the tares, and destroy those of his works which we feel he would have destroyed himself.

VERLAINE: I see.

ISABELLE: We were amazed, in fact, that the poems in *The Reliquary* were thought to be worthy of publication. We supposed that they could only have been published for motives of profit. I'd be very interested to know who pocketed the author's royalties.

VERLAINE (*guiltily*): Yes . . . well, er, I couldn't tell you.

ISABELLE: Here's my mother's card. Perhaps you could send the manuscripts to this address.

VERLAINE: As a matter of fact, Vanier and I were planning an edition of Rimbaud's complete works.

ISABELLE: Yes, M. Vanier told me.

VERLAINE: Well, don't you think that there's . . . a place for the works you mentioned in our edition? I mean, surely his conversion becomes even more striking if it's seen against . . . some of the things he wrote when he was young.

ISABELLE: I'm sure these considerations will be borne in mind.

VERLAINE: Yes, yes, of course. . . .

ISABELLE: I wonder if you could give me your address, so that I can get in touch with you if it's necessary.

VERLAINE: Well, I . . . don't really have an address, mademoiselle. I spend a lot of time in hospital, you see, and my address seems to . . . change quite often.

ISABELLE: I see. Well, I think that's about all, M. Verlaine.

VERLAINE: It occurs to me, that if you want Rimbaud's manuscripts, my wife might be able to help you.

ISABELLE: Your wife?

VERLAINE: Yes. I still think of her as my wife, although I'm told she's taken advantage of the Gospel according to the Civil Service, and married someone else. I haven't seen her since before . . . for about twenty years. I spent years trying to get her to send me Rimbaud's manuscripts and letters. I don't know where she lives now, but I should imagine you could get hold of her if you wanted to. Perhaps you'd have

78

better luck than I did.

ISABELLE: Yes. Thank you.

VERLAINE: She's a spiteful and wicked woman. Do you know that my son will be twenty-one this year, and I haven't seen him since he was eight?

ISABELLE: I think I should be going, M. Verlaine, I'd like to get back to my hotel before it gets dark.

VERLAINE: Wait. Please. Just a minute. I wonder if you could, before you go, just tell me something about . . . your brother. You see, the last time I saw him, in Stuttgart, must have been about seventeen years ago, when he was over there learning German. After that, the reports were so vague. We heard he was in Abyssinia, we heard he was dead, and later that he was alive, and all kinds of rumours. I wonder if you could just . . . fill in the details a little, that's all.

ISABELLE: I don't know that there's very much to tell. He travelled. He was a building consultant in Cyprus for some time, then he moved on to Aden and got a job with a trading firm. He established a new depot for them in Abyssinia about five years ago, which he managed and ran himself.

VERLAINE: But how did he die?

ISABELLE: He had a tumour on his knee.

VERLAINE: That's very strange.

ISABELLE: Why?

VERLAINE: Because that's what I have, a . . . tumour on my knee.

ISABELLE: It would have been all right if he'd done something about it sooner, if he hadn't been so conscientious about his work. There was no doctor there, but he insisted on staying until the pain became unbearable. After that, it took him two months to get back to Marseilles, and they amputated his leg—but by that time it was too late to do anything for him.

VERLAINE: How terrible.

ISABELLE: In fact, after the operation it was worse. They tried to fit him with a wooden leg, but he couldn't manage it. They'd

79

had to amputate too high and the stump couldn't take the weight. He said, after the operation, he kept saying, that if he'd known what it was going to be like, he'd never have let them amputate. He hated the hospital so much, that at the end of July he left and came home.

VERLAINE: Was he alone in Marseilles?

ISABELLE: Oh yes. Mother went down for the operation, but she couldn't afford to stay with him, because it was getting near to harvest-time.

(*A burst of raucous laughter from* EUGÉNIE.)

ISABELLE: When he got home things weren't too bad at first, but before long his health began to deteriorate. He lost the use of his right arm, and the pain spread and increased. The doctor gave him drugs to stop the pain, and he became delirious. I remember one night, I was woken up by a terrible crash from his room. I rushed up there and found my brother lying face down on the floor, naked. He told me he had opened his eyes and it was dawn, and time to go, to lead his caravan of ivory and musk to the coast. It was time to leave, and he had leapt out of bed. . . . After that, he refused to take any drugs again for a long time. He used to spend whole days crying.

VERLAINE: But I thought he died in Marseilles.

ISABELLE: Yes, he only stayed at home for a month. If you remember, it was a very bad summer—there was rain and fog, and the crops were ruined by frost. He kept saying that he wanted to go back to the sun, and that the sun would heal him, and eventually he left for Marseilles and I went with him. He intended to travel on from there to Aden, but when we got there he was too ill, and he went back into hospital. He was there nearly three months before he died, the paralysis gradually spread, and a large tumour appeared on the inside of his stump. They tried all kinds of things, massage, electric treatment, but it was no good. I think God kept him alive long enough to repent, so that he could be saved.

VERLAINE: Yes. The last time we met, in Stuttgart, we spoke of religion. I had just been converted, and I tried very hard to convince him of the truth. Perhaps I helped him in some small way.

(*Silence.* EUGENIE *exits on the arm of the man she has been talking to.*)

ISABELLE: It was only when he was dying that I realized he was a poet. When he was delirious, he spoke so gently and beautifully, that even the doctors came to listen. Often what he said made no sense, it was confused and strange, and sometimes he spoke in Arabic, but at the time it seemed perfectly easy to understand. He was in a coma for most of the last week, but on the day before he died he revived a little, and dictated a letter to a steamship company, booking a passage to Aden. He wanted the sun so much.

VERLAINE: Did he . . . I don't suppose he ever mentioned me.

ISABELLE: No. He spoke most often of Djami, his servant in Abyssinia, in fact he even left him some money in his will.

VERLAINE: It was a long time ago.

ISABELLE: It's getting dark. I must go.

VERLAINE: But still. . . .

(ISABELLE *stands up, and* VERLAINE, *at first startled by her movement, drags himself painfully to his feet.*)

ISABELLE: Good-bye, M. Verlaine.

(*They shake hands.*)

VERLAINE: Won't you let me see you to your hotel?

ISABELLE: No, it's quite all right.

VERLAINE: Are you sure?

ISABELLE (*formally*): It was an honour to meet such a distinguished poet.

VERLAINE: It was a great pleasure to meet you, mademoiselle.

ISABELLE: You have mother's card there, don't you? Don't forget to send us Arthur's manuscripts.

VERLAINE: No.

ISABELLE: Good-bye, monsieur.

VERLAINE: Good night.

(*Exit* ISABELLE. VERLAINE *sits down. For a moment there is absolute silence. Then he tears up* MME RIMBAUD's *visiting card, smiling a little to himself.*)

Eugénie? Where are you?

Absinthe. Two, please.

(*The* BARMAN *pours two absinthes into the two glasses already on the table.* VERLAINE *drinks.*)

It was a long time ago. But I remember the first time I saw him. That evening in the Mautés' main room. When we walked in, he was standing with his back to us, looking out of the window. He turned round and spoke, and then I saw him, and I was amazed how beautiful he was. He was sixteen.

Since he died I see him every night. My great and radiant sin.

(RIMBAUD *enters, dressed as he was in the first scene, but moving with more confidence, smiling, handsome, lithe. He sits down at the table next to* VERLAINE *and they smile at each other.*)

Tell me if you love me.

RIMBAUD: You know I'm very fond of you. We've been very happy sometimes.

(*Silence.*)

Do you love me?

VERLAINE: Yes.

RIMBAUD: Then put your hands on the table.

VERLAINE: What?

RIMBAUD: Put your hands on the table.

(VERLAINE *does so.*)

Palm upwards.

(VERLAINE *turns his hands palm upwards.* RIMBAUD *looks at them for a moment, and then bends forward and kisses them. Then he gets up, smiles at* VERLAINE, *and exits. There is a long silence.*)

VERLAINE: We were always happy. Always. I remember.

(VERLAINE *sits alone in a pool of light, which gradually dims as he speaks.*)

Eugénie?

What I love in old, sad flesh is the youth which whispers around it. I love its memories of youth.

I remember our first summer, how happy it was, the happiest time of my life. Wandering across Belgium, eating turnips and huddling in ditches. He's not dead, he's trapped and living inside me. As long as I live, he has some kind of flickering and limited life. It's always the same words and the same gestures—the same images: I walk behind him across a steep ploughed field; I sit, talking to him in a darkening room, until I can barely see his profile and his expressive hand; I lie in bed at dawn and watch him sleeping and see how nervously his hand brushes at his cheek. I remember him of an evening and he lives.

Absinthe.

Are you there? Eugénie? Are you there?

(*Darkness.*)

CURTAIN

APPENDIX

Extract from one of Rimbaud's last letters to his sister:

Marseilles, 15th July, 1891.

My dear Isabelle,

. . . I spend day and night torturing myself, trying to think of ways to get about. I want to do all kinds of things, live, get away from here: but it's impossible, at least, it'll be impossible for months, if not for ever. All I can think about are these damn crutches: without them, I can't take a step, I can't exist. I can't even get dressed without the most terrible gymnastics. It's true I can run now with my crutches; but I can't go up or down stairs, and if the ground isn't level, shifting the strain from one shoulder to the other is very tiring. I still have very painful neuralgia in my right arm and shoulder, and in addition to this, the crutches cut into my armpits. My left leg is very painful as well—and the worst thing is having to behave like an acrobat all day to have any sort of existence at all.

My dear sister, I've been thinking about what really caused my illness. The climate in Harar is cold from November to March. I never used to wear many clothes—just a pair of canvas trousers and a cotton shirt. Also I quite often used to walk 15 to 40 kilometres a day, leading lunatic processions across steep, mountainous country. I think I must have developed some arthritic trouble caused by fatigue and the heat and the cold. It all started with a kind of hammer blow which used to strike me under the kneecap every so often. The joint was very dry and my thigh was stiff. The next thing was the veins all round the knee swelled up, which made me think they were varicose. I kept on going for walks, and working harder than ever, I thought it was just a chill. Then the pain inside my knee got worse, every step I took, it was like a nail being driven in. I was still walking, but it got more and more difficult; so I used to ride, and whenever I dismounted, I felt completely crippled. Then the back of my knee swelled up, my kneecap got very fleshy, so did my shin. The blood wasn't circulating properly, and my nerves throbbed from my ankle right the way up to my back. I couldn't walk without a heavy limp, and it was getting worse and worse. But I still had a lot of essential work to do. I started bandaging the whole of my leg, massaging it, bathing it, and so on, but it was no good. I lost my appetite. I was suffering from stubborn insomnia. I got weaker and lost a lot of weight. About the 15th March, I decided to stay in bed between my desk and papers and the window, so that I could keep an eye on the scales at the end of the yard, and I paid people to keep the business going, while I lay there with my leg stretched out. Every day the knee swelled up more until it was like a large ball. I noticed that the back of the shin bone was much bigger at the top than on the other leg. I couldn't move the kneecap, it was soaked in the muck which formed the swelling, which, I was horrified to see, turned as hard as bone within a few days. A week later, my whole leg was stiff, I couldn't bend it at all; I had to drag myself along the ground to the latrines. In the meantime my calf and my thigh got thinner and thinner, while the knee joint swelled, hardened, and seemed to turn into bone; and my physical and mental weakness increased. At the end of March, I decided to leave. I sold up everything in a few days—at a loss; and as the stiffness and pain prevented me from riding a mule or even a camel, I had a litter made with a curtain roof, and hired 16 men, who took a fortnight to get me to Zeyla. On the second day of the journey, we went on far ahead of the caravan, and were caught in a rainstorm in the middle of the desert. I lay for 16 hours in the pouring rain, with no shelter and no possibility of movement; this did me a great deal of harm. On the way I was never able to get out of the litter. They set up the tent above me wherever they'd happened to put me down. I used to dig a hole with my hands near the edge of the litter, crawl over to it with great difficulty, relieve myself into it, and then fill it with earth again. In the morning they'd take the tent away; then they'd take me away. I arrived at Zeyla exhausted and paralysed. I had only four hours' rest there before the steamer left for Aden. They bundled me on to the bridge on my mattress, having hoisted me aboard in my litter, and I had to endure three days at sea without eating. Then I spent a few days settling things with M. Tian and left for the hospital where the English doctor advised me, a fortnight later, to push off back to Europe.

I'm absolutely certain that if the pain in the joint had been treated at once, it could easily have been cured and would have had no consequences. But I had no idea how serious it was, and I ruined everything by insisting on long walks and hard work.

Why don't they teach medicine at school, at least enough to prevent people from making such stupid mistakes?

If anyone, in the condition in which I then found myself, came to me for advice, I would say to him: however bad it is, never let them amputate. If you die, it will be better than living with a missing limb. People often refuse, and if I had another chance, I would. Better to suffer the tortures of hell for a year than to let them amputate!

Anyway, they have. And this is the result. Most of the time I'm sitting down, but every so often, I get up, hop a hundred yards or so on my crutches, and then sit down again. My hands can't grip. When I'm walking, I can't take my eyes off my only foot and the end of the crutches. My head and shoulders bend forward and I look like a hunchback. I'm frightened of things and people moving around me, in case they knock me over and break my other leg. People watch me hopping and snigger. When I sit down again, my hands are limp, my armpits are bruised, my expression is vacuous. I despair; and I sit here, completely powerless, snivelling, and waiting for the night, which will bring me the same endless insomnia until the dawn of a day still more miserable than the last. So it goes on.

I will write again soon.

All best wishes,
RIMBAUD

SELECTED BIBLIOGRAPHY

Album Rimbaud: ed. Pierre Petitfils and Henri Matarasso, Bibliothèque de la Pléiade, 1967

Rimbaud: *Oeuvres Complètes*, ed. Roland de Renéville and Jules Mouquet, Bibliothèque de la Pléiade, 1965

Verlaine: *Oeuvres Poétiques Complètes*, ed. Jacques Borel, Bibliothèque de la Pléiade, 1965

Delahaye, Ernest: *Souvenirs Familiers*, Messein, 1925

Lepelletier, Edmond: *Paul Verlaine, sa vie, son oeuvre*, Mercure de France, 1907

Martino, Pierre: *Verlaine*, Boivin, 1924

Mouquet, Jules: *Rimbaud raconté par Verlaine*, Mercure de France, 1934

Porché, Francois: *Verlaine tel qu'il fut*, Flammarion, 1933

Rimbaud, Isabelle: *Reliques*, Mercure de France, 1922

Starkie, Enid: *Arthur Rimbaud*, Faber & Faber (3rd ed.), 1961

Verlaine, Ex-Madame: *Mémoires de ma vie*, Flammarion, 1935

Wilson, Edmund: *Axel's Castle*, Charles Scribner, 1931 (Fontana, 1961)